1972

Under-standing Micro-economics

ROBERT L. HEILBRONER

Under-standing Micro-economics

PRENTICE-HALL, INC.
ENGLEWOOD CLIFFS, NEW JERSEY

PRENTICE-HALL INTERNATIONAL, INC., London
PRENTICE-HALL OF AUSTRALIA, PTY. LTD., Sydney
PRENTICE-HALL OF CANADA, LTD., Toronto
PRENTICE-HALL OF INDIA PRIVATE LTD., New Delhi
PRENTICE-HALL OF JAPAN, INC., Tokyo

for Maurine Lewis

Preface

The very worst way to introduce a subject is to be defensive about it: nonetheless, I shall take that tack in this introduction to Microeconomics. The reason is that our subject has been put in the shade (at least in the minds of many beginning students) by the flashier reputation of its younger brother, Macroeconomics. Macroeconomics — so goes the current report — is where the action is, where the really exciting questions lie. Microeconomics is just the part of economics you take to get credit for the course.

Happily for those who are about to plunge into a first engagement with microeconomics, I can report that its lesser reputation has no basis in fact. Indeed, I am inclined to think that many of the most highly charged political and social questions of today and tomorrow lie not in the area of macro- but of microanalysis. The repair of poverty, the rescue of the cities, the beautification of the countryside, the distribution of income, the problem of labor unions and of giant corporations — all these critical issues fall within the province of micro- rather than macro-economics.

Moreover, there is an even deeper reason for the relevance and importance of our subject. It is that all the "exciting" questions with which macroeconomics deals — inflation or recession or growth — turn out, upon close examination, to be curiously elusive concepts. There is no such *thing* as a depression or a boom — there are only collections of statistics that describe the outcome of the activities of thousands of individuals and firms. This is not to deny for an instant the enormous importance of these abstractions, but to point out that all the "big" questions of macro-analysis are ultimately rooted in the realities of individual behavior on which microeconomics turns its analytical gaze. To put it differently, we cannot really understand the behavior and misbehavior of our macro system until we have looked very carefully into the behavior and misbehavior of the micro system, which is to say, into ourselves.

Thus microeconomics can provide the key, not only to an understanding of economics, but to the role we play in economic society itself. It would be a disservice, however, to pretend that this key will drop into your hands by the mere act of turning these pages and dutifully scrutinizing their contents. Economics is in many ways a demanding discipline that requires more than a passive attitude from those who seek to master it. Hence let me add a few teacherly comments that may simplify the task ahead.

To begin with, economics speaks a special language, and as with all new tongues, it is easy to make careless (but grievous) mistakes because a strange vocabulary has not been mastered. Many new students, for the first time coming upon an italicized term such as *quantity demanded*, are sure that the author really meant *demand* instead, and so they use the short word for the cumbersome phrase and wonder why their quizzes come back with red X's. It is not mere pedantry that motivates your instructor in thus marking you down. Words in economics, as in all specialized inquiries, have very precisely defined meanings, and small deviations from those words can bring large discrepancies in the sense of what one says. Hence I must caution you to pay careful attention to the way things are said, even though this is often a bother. The new vocabulary will not be a hurdle if you make up your mind to speak it carefully, but it can present a monumental burden if you neglect to learn it right the first time.

Second, microeconomics comes replete with myriad diagrams. To most students these diagrams are rather enjoyable; to a few they are as undecipherable as Minoan Linear B. For the baffled, I can only counsel patience or resignation, but for the large majority I must advise the habit of learning to draw with loving care the revealing, marvelously helpful diagrammatic aids. Diagrams are worth a thousand words of text, all right—but only when they *are* right. Hence look carefully at where curves touch and cross and draw yours the same way.

There is one easy way to master this bit of the economist's art. It is to understand that the diagrams are representations of quantitative relationships that really exist in the world, not merely figments of an artist's imagination. The objective is to understand *why* line AB touches curve CD at point X, and not at Y or Z; for once you see the real processes of which these diagrams are only schematic representations, you will not make the lines and curves do things they shouldn't.

The subject of diagrams brings me to the last and most important admonition. As I have written before in reference to macroeconomics,* a student entering microeconomics must be prepared for a subject that is tinged with a considerable degree of abstraction. This is not a synonym for dullness or difficulty. Abstraction means that a problem is taught in its greatest possible degree of generality, so that what we learn can be applied to as many cases as possible. It may seem more urgent to study a problem, such as poverty, by poring over the detailed facts of a particular instance of it — studying, let us say, the grim facts of a particular block in Harlem. But the consequence of such a course is that we are apt to apply our conclusions to another block in another city, only to find that they do not apply there at all.

What economics tries to do is to back away from the individual case — not to minimize its human aspects, but to see it as an instance of a broader set of circumstances. Only in that way can we hope to find remedies that will apply to the *causes* of problems as well as to their symptoms. Abstraction is thus not the "trouble" with economics; it is its very point.

But this is enough by way of defensiveness. My final word must be in another key. Microeconomics is the real inner structure of economics, and economics to my prejudiced belief is the most adventurous and absorbing of all the social sciences. When we deal with economics, we take our society in miniature and hold it in our own hands, to examine it as if it were a man-made artifact. Then comes the stunning realization: that is precisely what it is. Microeconomics gives us a jeweler's lens to look at what we ourselves have made. We may or may not be pleased with what we see, but no other study gives us so clear a feeling that it is our own condition that we are learning to understand and control.

ROBERT L. HEILBRONER

---

*I must append a word on the origin of this book. Some years ago I began a long text, since published as *The Economic Problem*, in which both macro- and microtheory were to be presented in a general framework of economic history. As the first portions of the text, on history and macroanalysis, were finished, each was published as an independent volume (with some changes to make them self-sufficient), and each found a niche for itself in various curricula. Accordingly, the present text has also been taken from *The Economic Problem* and given its independence, in the hope that it will also prove useful for those instructors who like to teach their courses from a wide variety of sources rather than from one book alone.

Introduction

What is microeconomics all about?

Let us answer the question by supposing that you are a general in command of an occupying army and that your task is to provide for the needs of a city in a nation where all economic activity has come to a disastrous halt.

The first thing to be done, of course, is to feed the city's population. Accordingly, you would quickly arrange for a census, and draw up a list of essential foodstuffs, showing the amounts of different items required. Then you would send your men out into the countryside to buy (or if necessary to commandeer) the grains, dairy products, meat, and so on.

Immediately you would find that you also need an immense network of transportation. Some of the food your men would earmark for the city would no doubt lie on farms at the periphery of the city, but if the urban center were large, you would have to go many miles before you could round up supplies enough for the coming months. Hence you would soon have to collect a fleet of barges, trucks, rail transportation, etc., to bring in the requisitioned provisions. Next you would arrange to have this huge fleet fueled and maintained and manned so that the operation of supply could be set into motion.

Last, within the city itself you would have to plan for the final phase of the operation. Collection points would have to be established, where food could be cleaned, stored, refrigerated, processed, packaged; and a subfleet of local delivery vehicles would have to be rounded up to bring the provisions to distribution points where the populace itself could finally obtain them.

Complex logistical operations like this have often been carried out—many cities in occupied territories were kept going by similar methods during and after World War II. Yet it is hardly surprising that such economic systems (for that is what they are) rarely work smoothly. The original calculations of the needs of the population frequently contain serious errors. The commandeering of supplies can lead to violence. The coordination of a vast transportation network almost inevitably brings confusion and delay. Inside the city the distribution of food is apt to be marked by long queues and strict rationing.

But with all its problems, the task of maintaining a city for a few months or even a year can be solved with reasonable effectiveness. Suppose, however, that your orders were now changed, making you responsible for the city for the next ten years. Instantly you would have to extend the reach of your authority. The farmers from whom you have gathered your supplies for one season must now be instructed how much to plant or raise for the next—indeed for the next ten seasons. Meanwhile, your transportation adviser warns you that by next year much of your transportation equipment will be badly worn, and that within ten years nearly all of it will be unusable. The officer in charge of city distribution adds that the local delivery fleet will also need replacement and that some of the food storage and processing equipment is on its last legs.

Hence you begin to draw up plans for maintaining or expanding all this essential equipment. But now another problem arises. An economist on your staff points out that if you are to place orders for vehicles of various kinds, you will also have to see that the companies that manufacture these vehicles are themselves properly supplied with the materials and equipment *they* will need to fulfill your orders. But this in turn draws you still deeper into the maze. For the companies that make the materials and equipment that will be needed by the companies that make trucks or freight cars require in turn their own inputs of special kinds of material and equipment. And like an infinite series of images reflected in two facing mirrors, those industries will also require the output of still other industries if they are to fulfill the demands put on them.

The problem begins to stagger us. But we have not yet even begun to itemize its full complexity. Not only materials but labor must be provided for each stage of the interlocked production process. This labor will require housing and food, which may have to be routed to new destinations if the labor force is to be relocated to take care of the new equipment you have ordered. And then, of course, there is the obvious fact that a city does not live on food alone. Fuel, chemicals, building materials, clothing supplies, power must also pour into the city to sustain its daily life; and each of these items has its own endlessly long chain of suppliers (each of whom must be supplied), and each has its own requirements for labor, fully as complex as the one we have mentioned.

The problem begins to seem insuperable, even fanciful. Who could possibly make the uncountable calculations and decisions that coordinate all these interdependent actions into one smoothly operating whole?

Tradition, command, and market

Surprising as it may be, however, the problem is neither imaginary nor beyond solution. In fact, not only the economies of occupied countries, but all economic systems everywhere must solve economic problems, often of just this degree of complexity and bafflement. Moreover, as the continued existence both of cities and larger economic systems testifies, the problem *is* solved in some fashion or other, although not always very well.

How is it done? For all the variety of detail from one economy to another, *we can discern but three methods — three techniques — of solving it.*

The first is by using *tradition* as the guiding principle by which the economy organizes itself. Under such a system, tasks are performed with but little change from generation to generation, and life thus proceeds along its well-worn rut in a changeless pattern of succession. Tradition, it need hardly be said, is not a solution that lends itself well to fast-changing industrial life. We mainly find it as the great regulator of economic activity in the less economically developed countries of the world.

A second mode resembles very much our example of the occupation army. It is the mode of *command* — a means of solving the economic problem that we can trace back as far as the Pharaohs, and as far forward as the planned economies of the Soviet Union or China. Command systems, unlike those based on tradition, are by no means wedded to changelessness. Command is often the means by which vast and dislocating changes are imposed on society; for example, changes that bring tradition-bound systems into the industrial orbit. But command, as our example suggests, has problems of its own. The difficulties and frictions of planning and coordinating the incredible variety of different kinds of output needed to supply an economy over time are staggeringly large. Hence inefficiency, waste, and bureaucracy are all too frequently found as the counterparts of command. However valuable as an instrument of large-scale economic change, it is a crude means of assuring the smooth running and continuous adjustment of a society that is not seeking to alter itself radically.

And what is the third method? The answer, we know, is the *market system* — that extraordinary interplay of buying and selling from which the solution to the provisioning challenge arises so "effortlessly" that we cease even to be aware of the challenge itself. This is not to say, as we shall see in greater detail in this book, that the market system is a perfect answer to the ubiquitous economic problem of provisioning. In the cities and nations where the market takes the place of tradition and command, there are some who have too little and some who have too much; there are transportation delays and failures in retail distribution; and there are even partial breakdowns in the system itself, so that production may decline and men may be unable to find work although there is no decline in society's wants and needs, nor in its citizens' desire to work.

Yet with all its failures, the market system provides a truly remarkable solution to the economic problem. Unlike the systems guided by tradition, it imposes no restraining hand on change; indeed, no system breeds innovation and invention so prodigiously as the market. Unlike the system of command, it depends on no imposed authority or bureaucratic supervision over economic life. On the contrary, the very essence of the market system is its ability to bring about economic order and progress in what seems to be a condition of utter freedom for the participants in the process. Dynamic, flexible, self-regulating, self-correcting—and at the same time open to dangers and difficulties that the systems of tradition and command do not experience—the market is one of the most sophisticated and remarkable institutions to arise in history.* Our task in this book will be to discover how it works.

---

*We cannot here go into the story of how the market did arise. Let no student think, however, that it represents a "natural" form of economic organization that springs up spontaneously everywhere. Societies organized on the market principle are confined to a very small span of historic time and to a narrow portion of the globe. Indeed, the market system may well be a unique creature of Western civilization that will never again be wholly duplicated, although there is no doubt that many of its features will appear in time in the tradition-bound and command-run societies that are now striving to surpass the market-run Western world. Someone who is interested in this profoundly important and interesting problem might look into an earlier book of mine, *The Making of Economic Society,* 2nd ed. (Englewood Cliffs, N.J.: Prentice-Hall, Inc., 1968).

Contents

1

The tasks of the market system

How does the market solve the problem that was so baffling to us as vicarious authorities of a command economy? It will take us the full span of this book to answer the question with any degree of thoroughness. But at the very outset it may help us to organize the problem in our minds if we apply the very method of abstraction for which we have been readied. Hence, instead of looking more closely into the details of the transactions that constitute the lifeblood of the market process, let us first back away from the bustle of the marketplace and ask a basic question: What are the social functions that *any* economic mechanism — be it run by tradition, command, or the market — must carry out?

If we think about such a question, we can see that there are three tasks that all such economic mechanisms must perform.

1. *All economic systems must allocate the effort of society to the production of the goods and services needed by that society.* Whether they are run by tradition, command, or market, all societies must be able to count on the regular output of the provisions they need. In the case of a very simple economic society, such as the primitive Bushmen of South Africa, this may mean no more than that the tribe have enough men to hunt and enough women to gather plants to be able to support itself in the never-ending search for food. In advanced societies, the "necessities" go far beyond food, as we have seen in the hypothetical case of the occupied city. Yet in principle, the task is the same: all societies rest on economic organizations that must allocate their men and materials to those uses that the community requires for its continued functioning. If the method of organization fails, the community will collapse.

2. *All economic systems must also determine the methods of production.* Production is not merely a matter of applying human effort to nature. In every social system, from the most primitive to the

1

most advanced, there is also the problem of what technique to use. The Bushmen, to take again the simplest of all economic societies, have long ago settled on the best means of hunting and the best methods of foraging, so that we rarely see this society in the act of choosing the better of two ways of going about something. But in virtually all societies above the level of subsistence, there is always the question of *how* to produce what society wants, as well as what to produce. As generals of an occupied city, for instance, we would have to decide what kinds of transportation equipment to order, what methods of farming to encourage, what sorts of distribution systems to build up. The wrong choice of technique may not bring collapse (although it might), as would an outright failure to allocate men and materials to their necessary uses, but it will entail waste and a lower level of well-being than was actually available to that society.

3. *All economic systems must solve the problem of distributing output among its members.* In many ways this is the most difficult problem of all. For in all societies, including our own (which is by far the world's wealthiest), the prevailing fact is the inadequacy of output to fulfill the community's wants. *Scarcity* — whether imposed by nature or attributable to human appetites — is the obdurate reality of economic life; and scarcity makes the solution to the problem of dividing up output extremely demanding. Yet, whether by custom, command, or otherwise, if society is to go on, the inadequate output of the system must be shared — and in some manner that is acceptable.

How the market works

Thus *what* to produce, *how* to produce it, and *to whom* to give it constitute the basic questions of economics with which every social order must cope in one way or another.

But how does the market deal with these three questions? It seems not to pay heed to them at all. When first we look into a market system, all we see is an immense bargaining process in which every man is left to fend for himself, where no one is responsible for seeing to it that the right goods will be produced, that they will be produced in the right way or given to the right people.

It may help us to understand this puzzle if we look at the tasks of the market once again, in a somewhat different light. Suppose we have an island where we can make only two kinds of output. We can use our land, labor, and capital to raise grain or we can use them to raise cattle for milk. Now suppose that we used all of our resources for grain production for one year and found that we could raise 1,000 tons of grain. The following

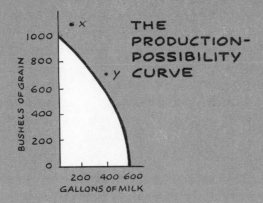

FIG. 1-1

year, we put our whole effort into dairy farming and discovered that we netted 500 gallons of milk. We would now have discovered two extreme production possibilities for the allocation of our social effort.

But the chances are that we would prefer to have a mixture of grain and milk, rather than all of one and none of the other. Hence we would have to find out, by experimenting, what combinations of grain and milk we could enjoy by using some of our resources for each occupation. Fig. 1-1 shows us what kind of *production-possibility curve* we might in fact have.

The production-possibility curve

The production-possibility curve shows us a number of things. First it makes vivid the material meaning of the word *scarcity*. Any point outside the frontier of the curve is unattainable for our island community, given its present resources. This is obviously true of point X. But look at point Y. This is an output that represents roughly 700 bushels of grain and 400 gallons of milk. Either one of these goals, taken separately, lies well within the production possibilities of the island. What the curve shows us is that *we cannot have both at the same time.* If we want 700 bushels of grain, we must be content with less than 400 gallons of milk; and if we want 400 gallons of milk, we will have to settle for about 600 bushels of grain. Thus we see that *at the core of the production problem lies the necessity for choice.* This unavoidable choice is imposed, of course, by the existing resources and our technical knowledge. But the frontier of possibilities is not static. As capital and knowledge grow, the frontier can advance, so that what was impossible in the past becomes attainable in the future, as Fig. 1-2 shows.

Furthermore, as techniques change, or as our resources become more developed or depleted, the frontier of choice also changes. For instance, the invention of a new cattle fodder might raise the production possi-

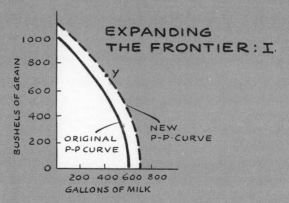

FIG. 1-2

bility of milk on our island. Then our production-possibility curve would look like Fig. 1-3.*

We could now easily produce 700 bushels of grain and 400 gallons of milk — in fact, more of either or more of both. But the location of point *Y* in Fig. 1-3 makes clear another meaning of the *p-p* curve. The curve shows our production possibilities *when we use our resources fully*. If we fail to employ all our land, labor, and capital (or if we use them ineffectively), we will end up with a collection of goods, such as *Y*, which falls short of our potential.

From production possibilities to market actualities

The production-possibility curve gives a fresh meaning to the tasks of the market, in particular to the questions of what goods to produce and how to produce them. It makes us see that economics is basically concerned with choices and decisions that result in different levels and assortments of output.

But there is something of a puzzle in the contrast between the pro-

*The alert student may have noticed that all the production-possibility curves have bowed shapes. The reason for this lies in the *changing efficiency* of our resources as we shift them from one use to another. When we are concentrating all our resources on grain, for example, we have to use some land, labor, and capital that would be much better suited to producing milk. Hence the initial transfer of some resources out of grain and into milk gives us a relatively larger gain in milk than our loss in grain — which is why the curve at this end of the graph slopes "milkward" rather than "grainward." At the other end of the curve, just the opposite considerations prevail. Now we have to cram into milk production the last units of resources that must be withdrawn from the grain production to which they are better suited. Hence, here the gain in milk output is proportionately much less than at the other end of the scale, and the loss in grain output proportionately much more. Therefore the curve now slopes more sharply in the direction of grain than milk. The actual shapes of production-possibility curves may have considerably different contours, but the law of increasing costs makes most of them bowed, or concave from below. Note that their shape is entirely determined by technological or physical considerations. We will understand more of this when we study the law of diminishing returns in Chapter 6.

4

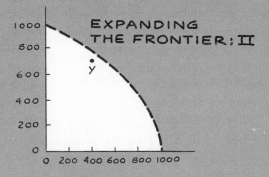

FIG. 1-3

duction-possibility diagram with its clear-cut outline of economic choice and the milling confusion of the marketplace. We turned to the production-possibility curve to clarify the tasks that the market as a system was to perform. But we have yet to understand how a particular point X or Y on the diagram is brought into being. Who decides whether society will use its resources for milk or grain, or what combination of them? Who determines whether society will operate on the frontier of its potential or will suffer the consequences of a less-than-full use of resources?

The answer, of course, is the interaction of individuals and firms we call the market system. Thus we study the market mechanism to learn about not only the potentialities of a system, but about its actualities, for microeconomics will teach us how the financial exchanges of buyers and sellers bring about the level and composition and disposition of output in our society.

The factors of production

How does the market, with its immense confusion of individuals and firms, determine the allocation of society's resources? If we are to answer this question we will have to disentangle the market's activities and discover in its flux some pattern that will allow us to grasp how it works.

Is there such a pattern? Indeed there is. For if we look again at the flux of the marketplace, we can see that not all the participants are alike. In fact, the first clue to the operation of the market system comes when we see that there are both *two kinds of participants* and *two locales* in the seemingly undifferentiated market.

One group of participants is instantly recognizable to us. It consists of individuals, like ourselves, who enter the market as buyers, to provide themselves with the goods and services they want or can afford. These are the *consumers*, whom we ordinarily think of as comprising the only — or anyway, the most important — group in the "market."

But if we look again we can see that they are not. There is a second

5

group, fully as large and important as the first, whose role we must now follow. These are the selfsame individuals whom we have already identified as consumers, this time entering the market for a different purpose: to earn a living by offering their services for production. Further, we can distinguish at least three kinds of services put forward by these individuals. One such service is *labor,* offered by individuals in a variety of forms, as untrained and low-paid as that of a porter, or as refined and highly paid as that of a chief executive. A second are the services of *natural resources, such as land,* which are offered by those individuals who own these resources. A third are the services of *capital* — man-made instruments of production — which are offered on the market by those who own these instruments.

We call all these individuals in their roles as producers *the factors of production,* and we can now see that they constitute a group and an activity that is in every way the equal of consumers in importance. The labor, land, and capital that are offered by the individuals who own their own skills, or who own resources or equipment, constitute not only the *physical agencies* of production that must be combined to secure output, but constitute also — we can now see — *social* classes whose behavior must be coordinated to bring about production. Or to put it differently, the market combines the actual physical realities of work, resources, and equipment by arranging for the appropriate activities of those who own each of these physical entities.*

Thus the market becomes something more than a milling confusion. It is now a place where consumers and factors of production each search for the solution to *their* particular and individual problems, spending their incomes to satisfy their personal wants on the one hand, and earning money by offering their skills or possessions on the other.

The two markets

Moreover, it is suddenly apparent that these two activities are themselves linked. The money that individuals spend as consumers is earned by them when they act as factors of production. *A great circle of transactions thus binds together in the market the participants who are buyers and those who are sellers.*

---

*Where and how did these individuals come into their various possessions? The question takes us into an investigation of the origin of the market system and of capitalism in particular. There are searching questions to be asked about the genesis and justification of a social order in which private individuals are permitted to own and control resources and the means of production, but these questions should not interfere with our purpose here, which is to learn how such a system works.

And with the awareness of this interconnection of consumers and factors, another aspect of the market clarifies itself for us. It is that two activities (the buying by individuals and the selling of factor services) take place in the market and that these activities take place in *two markets*. The individuals who are shopping for their private satisfactions are visitors to a part of the market in which the transactions involve goods and services. The individuals who are looking for a place to earn incomes are visitors to a part where the transactions are exclusively

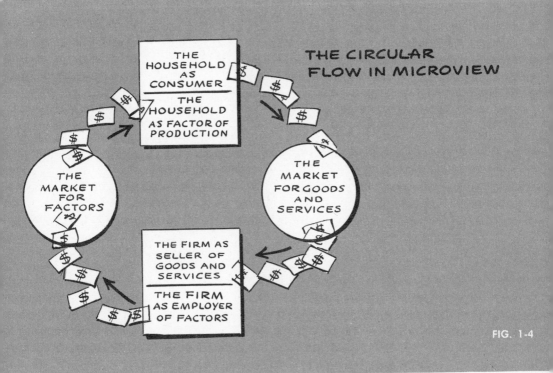

THE CIRCULAR FLOW IN MICROVIEW

THE HOUSEHOLD AS CONSUMER

THE HOUSEHOLD AS FACTOR OF PRODUCTION

THE MARKET FOR FACTORS

THE MARKET FOR GOODS AND SERVICES

THE FIRM AS SELLER OF GOODS AND SERVICES

THE FIRM AS EMPLOYER OF FACTORS

FIG. 1-4

concerned with the services of other individuals like themselves. One does not buy land, labor, or capital in a department store, or consumer goods and services at an employment agency or a real estate office or a bank.

Only one last aspect of the market remains to be clarified in this first approach. It is that the market system embraces not only individual participants, whether consumers or factors, but also an exceedingly important *institution*. This is the institution we call the firm, or the basic unit of business enterprise.

What is the role played by the firm? If we look one last time at the market, we can see that it is a central one. For in the part of the market where individuals are searching for goods and services, we see that the sellers of those goods and services are largely firms. And if we look across to the other side of the market where the factors of production are offering their services, we see that the buyers in that market are the very same firms. Thus, firms serve as the links in the circular chain we have already noticed, *buying* the services of land, labor, and capital and *selling* goods and services.

Figure 1-4 helps us visualize this circular flow of transactions. But more than that, it tells us how we can analyze the complexity of the market process. Rather than plunge into the confusion of the market as a system that is solving the economic problem by the interplay of innumerable activities, let us follow the easier route offered by the conception of a circular process. First we must learn about the market for goods and services, for this must certainly be connected with the task of assuring the community of its necessary output. Then we must proceed to the market for factors, for certainly the result of this market will give us insight into the question of who will be able to claim those goods and services. And last we investigate the central institution of the firm, for here is the focus of energy and organization in which the techniques of society are determined.

Thus to trace the interconnections of the circular flow will not only teach us how the market works, but it will bring us in a systematic fashion to the question we are now setting out to answer: How does the market system solve the economic problem?

Summary

1. Microeconomics *is an approach* to economics that begins with the actions of *individuals and firms* in the market process.
2. The market is a system for the solution of the basic economic problems of *production* and *distribution*. We can visualize the basic production tasks of the market by means of a *production-possibility diagram*.
3. The market brings about the dispositions of the real economy through a *network of transactions*. We can simplify this network into a *circular flow*, similar to that in the microeconomy.
4. The circular flow reveals the critical points at which the market performs its tasks—the *market for goods and services, the market for factors*, and the *internal workings of the firm*.

Questions

1. What is meant by the market as a *system*?
2. Describe the circular flow as it appears from the micro viewpoint.
3. What is the difference between the market for goods and that for factor services? On which market is the household a seller? The firm a seller? Can household and firm both be on the same side of the same market?

2

*The market
for goods*

The market for goods is the part of the market system
with which we are all most familiar, for we constantly enter it as pur-
chasers of commodities.* Now we must scrutinize this market to learn
how it actually works—to discover not only how prices are formed by
transactions of individuals and firms, but also how these prices, once
formed, help carry out the allocatory tasks of the market system as a
whole.

Everyone knows, whether or not he has taken a course
in economics, that prices in the market reflect "supply and demand."
When the price of milk goes up, we all say that the demand for milk
must have risen for some reason or other, or that the supply of milk
must have been cut. But this very general appreciation of the "forces" at
work only begins to explain how prices are actually determined, and tells
us nothing about how these prices in turn affect our own behavior.

Behavior and prices

What is the meaning of supply and demand? Our ac-
quaintance with the rise of market society tells us a good deal about the

*For many years, the late E. H. Chamberlain used to enliven his
famous course at Harvard on the workings of the market by dividing his students into
"sellers" and "buyers," giving to each person secret instructions about the price range he
was allowed to operate within. Thereafter the students were loosed into a free-for-all, each
to make bargains with the other side as best he could. As each buyer and seller reached
accord, their agreed-upon price was shown to Professor Chamberlain. At the end of the
session, the average of the prices reached in the classroom was compared with the average
of the price options given out. Chamberlain noted that the class result was regularly *under*
the true average of buying and selling options, and he hypothesized that this was due to the
superior skill his students had already accumulated as buyers, and their relative unfamili-
arity with the role of seller.

11

kind of behavior the terms describe. We remember that the emergence of the market system forced individuals to shift for themselves in a harsh world where private transactions determined both their incomes and their expenses. In such a world, sheer self-preservation dictated that buyers and sellers had to follow the arrow of price advantage if they were going to survive, much less prosper. Hence buying as cheaply as possible and selling as dearly as possible became the cardinal rule of behavior for both individuals and firms in a market setting. Added to this was the growing acceptance of economic gain as a primary goal of economic life, and the rule of Buy Cheap and Sell Dear was given a second social sanction.

Needless to say, these historic motives of self-preservation and economic gain have changed considerably as the market environment has changed from one of the extreme pressures of early capitalism to the far more sheltered setting of contemporary capitalism. Yet, albeit in the pursuit of somewhat altered objectives, we still usually behave as buyers by trying to spend as little as possible for the goods we want; and as sellers, by trying to get as much as we can for the goods and services we have to offer.

This clearly makes *the prices of goods* very important as stimuli that guide our behavior. Comparative prices enable us to make choices that will improve our economic position. But prices do more than this. *Prices also become signals that direct our behavior.* In fact, it is through our reaction to prices that self-interest becomes a "force" on the marketplace.

But since buyers and sellers have conflicting self-interests, how can this be? The answer is that the same price signal gives rise to *different* behavior, depending on which side of the market we are. A rising price will usually look bad for buyers but good for sellers. Falling prices will generally be in the self-interest of buyers (who can now satisfy their wants for less money), but against the self-interest of sellers (who will now get less return for their efforts). Thus we begin to see that the price mechanism may be the way of satisfying divergent interests, of bringing together parties whose economic gains lie in opposing directions. That is why microeconomics is sometimes called *price theory*.

The conditions of supply and demand

Let us explore this idea by looking more carefully into the actual considerations that guide me as a buyer or seller.

When I enter the market for goods, which I do virtually every time I walk along a street, two factors determine whether or not I will actually become a buyer and not just a window-shopper. The first factor is the *tastes and desires* that decide whether I am willing to spend my money on the things I see. The windows of shops are crammed with many things that I could afford to buy if I wanted to, but which I simply do not wish to own. Perhaps if they were very cheap, I might wish to buy them; or possibly I would not even want them if they were free. For such goods, for which my desires are too weak to motivate me, my demand is zero.

On the other hand, my tastes and desires alone by no means suffice to make me a buyer. The shop windows are also full of goods that I would very much like to own but that I cannot afford to buy because they are too expensive: my demand for Rolls Royces is also zero. Thus demand hinges on the *ability*—the possession of sufficient wealth or income—as well as on the *willingness* of the buyer. If it did not, the poor, whose wants are always very large, would constitute the greatest source of demand.

Note that my demand for goods depends on both my willingness and my ability to buy them *at their going price*. From this it follows that the amount of goods I will demand will change as their prices change. If I see a sports car for $10,000 I am likely to be neither willing nor able to make the purchase, whereas the same car at $5,000 would find me both a great deal more willing and much more able; and at $2,000, it might set me to wondering if perhaps I should not buy two.

In the same way, willingness and ability both enter the market force of supply. Many suppliers of goods would be *willing* to offer certain commodities or services at certain prices, but are unable to do so because they lack the skills or the access to certain materials. Other suppliers may be perfectly *able* to offer the commodity at that price but may be unwilling to do so because they would incur a loss by doing so, or because of some other disinclination. Once again, price enters into the middle of this decision. At $10,000 many enterprisers would be willing (although not all might be able) to produce sports cars; at $5,000 the willingness and ability would be much reduced; and at $2,000 no one might be prepared to supply a single car.

This simple dissection of the considerations behind buying and selling tells us a good deal: supply and demand are terms that indicate our willingness and ability to sell or buy certain quantities of goods at certain prices. *Supply and demand are thus concepts that link our market behavior with price.*

Marginal utility

There is a point to be cleared up here before we go on. We have no difficulty in understanding why our ability to buy a commodity should decline as the price rises or increase as the price falls—our wealth simply stretches further or less far. But why should our willingness be related to price?

Economists answer this question by postulating that as we increase the quantities that we own of any good (within a given time period), the pleasures and benefits derived from successive units of that good will decline. Hence we will be less and less willing to go on buying more and more of the same good, because its *marginal utility* – the increment of satisfaction we derive from each additional unit – will diminish.

Suppose for example that a man were dying of thirst on the Sahara. The marginal utility to him of a pint of water per day would be immense, and he would pay a vast sum for just one pint. So too, perhaps, for the second or third pint. But after a certain number of pints per day, the utility of the next pint begins to fall. If such a man has 40 or 50 pints of drinking water a day, the marginal utility of the 41st or the 51st may be next to nothing. This does not mean that the *total* utility he enjoys is less than that of a man who is desperately short of water; just the opposite. But the *addition* to his utility of still another pint will have fallen so low that he will be willing to pay only very little for it.

The notion of diminishing marginal utility also clears up another puzzle of economic life. This is why we are willing to pay so little for bread, which is a necessity for life, and so much for diamonds, which are not. The answer is that we have so much bread that the marginal utility of any loaf we are thinking of buying is very little, whereas we have so few diamonds that each carat has a very high marginal utility. If we were locked inside Tiffany's over a long holiday, the price we would offer for bread and diamonds after a few days would be very different from when we entered.

Quantities and schedules

This relationship between price and quantity yields a conception of demand and supply that is different from the one that we ordinarily carry about in our heads. We are used to thinking about demand, for instance, as denoting a single purchase at a single price, or supply as referring to the readiness of a storekeeper to sell a certain good at a given price.

But that is not the idea of supply and demand as these words describe the behavior that drives the market system. *Demand and supply in their proper economic sense refer to various quantities of goods or services that we are willing and able to buy (or sell) at various prices at a given time.*

In other words, demand and supply both refer to *functional* relationships, or to the interdependence of price and quantity. This is a condition of which we do not often become conscious, but an imaginary situation may bring out the essential point. Suppose that you went into a clothing store to buy shirts and were waited on by an inexperienced clerk. Having found some shirts you liked, you asked the price and were told they were five dollars. "Very well," you say, having consulted your state of mind and your pocketbook, "I'll take three of them."

The salesman is about to write up the order when he stops in embarrassment. "I'm sorry, sir," he says, "I'm afraid I got the price wrong. It should be six dollars."

At six dollars you may be able to buy the shirts, but we will assume that you are no longer willing to—they are "too expensive." But just as you are about to leave, the clerk reappears. "I'm wrong about the price again," he admits. "These are six dollar shirts, all right, but they're on sale, reduced to $4.50."

At the new price, you make another mental calculation. "Very well," you say, "I'll take four."

Our example is meant to illustrate an aspect of demand that we do not ordinarily encounter in real life, when prices rarely change so rapidly. This is the fact that our "demand" covers a whole range of different quantities that we are willing and able to buy at different prices at a given time, and not just one quantity that we do buy (or do not buy) at a given price.*

The same functional relationship is of course visible between price and the quantity we are willing and able to sell, but now the relationship goes the other way. A tailor, for example, might be willing to make ten shirts a day if he could sell them for $6 each, whereas if the price dropped to $5 he would make only 3, using his time to make other garments; and at $4.50 he would make none.

If we make a tabulation of the amounts of a commodity that will be bid for and offered at different prices, we present a *schedule* of demand and supply. For the example of shirts above it would look like Table 2-1.

TABLE 2 • 1

Price	Quantity demanded	Quantity supplied
$6.00	0	10
5.00	3	3
4.50	4	0

*Just for the sake of completeness, we ought to note that there is a class of so-called luxury goods for which the quantity demanded rises as their prices go up. The reason is that part of the utility of these goods is their price. It is not for nothing that Joy perfume advertises itself as "the most expensive perfume in the world." Its sales would probably fall sharply if it dropped its price and announced itself as "the second most expensive perfume in the world."

From here it is only a step to representing these schedules on graphs in the very convenient form of *demand and supply curves.* The schedules in Table 2-1 look like Fig. 2-1.

Perhaps we have already grasped the next step of our analysis. The fact that supply and demand schedules (or curves) show *contrary functional relationships* between prices and quantities suggests that from the interplay of these different market forces an equilibrium might be reached—a point at which price will balance the force of demand against that of supply. In the case below, this equilibrium price is obviously $5, since I will be willing and able to buy three shirts at that price and the tailor is willing and able to make them for me.

Individual and collective demand

Now we must add one last word before we continue our study of supply and demand. Thus far we have considered only the factors that make a single individual more willing and able to buy as prices fall, or less willing and able to sell. But generally when we speak of supply and demand we mean markets in which each side is composed of many suppliers and demanders. That gives us an additional reason for the slope of each curve. If we assume that most individuals have somewhat different willingnesses and abilities to buy, because their incomes and their marginal utilities are different; or that they have unequal willingnesses or abilities to sell, then we can see that *a change in price will bring into the market new buyers or sellers.* As price falls, for instance, it will trigger off the willingness or ability to buy of one person after another, thereby adding to the quantity of the good that will be purchased at that price; and conversely, as prices rise, the entry of sellers into the market will increase, and the quantity of goods they offer will rise accordingly.

DEMAND AND SUPPLY CURVES

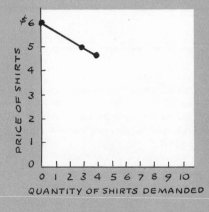
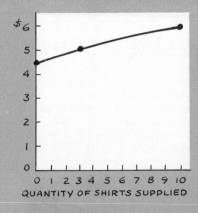

FIG. 2-1

Balancing supply and demand

Let us investigate a case of collective demand and collective supply by examining the supply and demand schedules for shoes for a small city over a period of a year. Suppose we discover that the price-quantity relationships look like Table 2-2.*

TABLE 2 • 2

Price	Quantity demanded (thousand pairs)	Quantity supplied (thousand pairs)
$50	1	125
45	5	90
40	10	70
35	20	50
30	25	35
25	30	30
20	40	20
15	50	10
10	75	5
5	100	0

As before, the schedules tell us that buyers and sellers react differently to prices. At high prices, buyers are either not willing or unable to purchase more than small quantities of shoes, whereas sellers would be only too willing and able to flood the city with them; at very low prices, the quantity of shoes demanded would be very great, but few shoemakers would be willing or able to gratify buyers at such low prices.

But if we now look at *both* schedules at *each* price level, we discover an interesting thing. *There is one price — $25 in our example — at which the quantity demanded is exactly the same as the quantity supplied.* At every other price, either one schedule or the other is larger, but at $25 the amounts in both columns are the same — 30,000 pairs of shoes. We call this balancing price the *equilibrium price,* and we shall soon see that it *is* the price that emerges spontaneously in an actual market where supply and demand contend.†

*Do these price–quantity relations have to be orderly and logical — that is, as the price falls by $5 increments, should demand or supply change in some regular fashion? The answer could be yes or no. In some markets, the relationship of demand or supply to price may be a very regular one; in others it is possible that reactions will be irregular and "illogical." This is a complicated subject, but it is well to be aware that demand and supply curves do not have to be as straight or smooth as they always appear in textbooks.

†Of course we have made up our schedules so that the quantities demanded and supplied would be equal at $25. The price that actually brought about such a balancing of supply and demand might be some odd number such as $25.01.

The emergence of the equilibrium price

How do we know that an equilibrium price will be brought about by the interaction of supply and demand? The process is one of the most important and fundamental in all of economics, so we should understand it very clearly.

Suppose in our example above that for some reason or other the shoe retailers in our city put a price tag on their shoes not of $25 but of $45. What would happen? Our schedules show us that at this price shoemakers will be pouring out shoes at the rate of 90,000 pairs a year, whereas customers would be buying them at the rate of only 5,000 pairs a year. Shortly, the shoe factories would be clogged with unsold merchandise. It is plain what the outcome of this situation must be. In order to realize some revenue, shoemakers will begin to unload their unsold stocks of shoes at lower prices.

As they do so, the situation will begin to improve. At a price of $40, demand picks up from 5,000 pairs to 10,000, while at the same time the slightly lower price discourages producers enough so that output falls from 90,000 pairs to 70,000. Shoemakers are still turning out more shoes than the market can absorb at the going price, but the difference between the quantities supplied and the quantities demanded is now smaller than it was before.

Let us suppose that the competitive pressure continues to reduce prices so that shoes soon sell at $30. Now a much more satisfactory state of affairs exists. Producers will be turning out 35,000 pairs of shoes, and consumers will be buying them at a rate of 25,000 a year. But still there is an imbalance, and some shoes will still be piling up, unsold, at the factory. Prices will therefore continue to fall. Eventually they reach $25. At this point, the quantity of shoes supplied by the manufacturers—30,000 pairs—is exactly that demanded by customers. There is no longer a surplus of unsold shoes hanging over the market and acting to press prices down. *The market clears.*

Now let us quickly trace the interplay of supply and demand from the other direction. Suppose that prices were originally $5. Our schedules tell us that customers would be standing in line at the shoe stores, but that producers would be largely shut down, unwilling or unable to make shoes at those prices. We can easily imagine that customers, many of whom would gladly pay more than $5, let it be known that they would welcome a supply of shoes at $10 or even more. If enough customers bid $10, a trickle of shoe output begins. But the quantity of shoes demanded at $10 far exceeds the available supply. Customers snap up the few pairs around, and shoe stores tell suppliers they could easily get $20 a pair. Prices rise accordingly. Now we are getting closer to a balance of quantities offered and bid for. At $20 there will be a demand for 40,000 pair of shoes and output will have risen to 20,000 pair. But still the pressure of unsatisfied demand raises prices further. Finally a price of $25 is tried. Now, once again, the quantities supplied and demanded are exactly in balance. There is no further pressure from unsatisfied customers to force the price up further, because at $25 no customer who can afford the price will remain unsatisfied.

The function of equilibrium prices

Thus we can see how *the interaction of supply and demand brings about the establishment of a price at which both suppliers and demanders are willing and able to sell or buy the same quantity of goods.* We can visualize the equilibrating process more easily if we now transfer our supply and demand schedules to graph paper. Figure 2-2 is the representation of the shoe market we have been dealing with.

The graph shows us at a glance the situation we have analyzed in detail. At the price of $25, the quantities demanded and supplied are equal—30,000 pair of shoes. But the graph also shows more vividly than the schedules why this is an *equilibrium* price.

Suppose that the price were temporarily lifted above $25. If you will draw a horizontal pencil line from any point on the vertical axis above the $25 mark to represent this price, you will find that it intersects the demand curve before it reaches the supply curve. In other words, *the quantity demanded is less than the quantity supplied at any price above the equilibrium price, and the excess of the quantity supplied means that there will be a downward pressure on prices, back toward the equilibrium point.*

The situation is exactly reversed if prices should fall below the equilibrium point. Now the quantity demanded is greater than that supplied, and the pressure of buyers will push the price up to the equilibrium point.

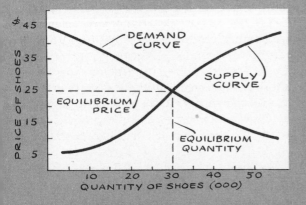

DETERMINATION OF AN EQUILIBRIUM PRICE

FIG. 2-2

Thus equilibrium prices have two important characteristics:

1. *They are the prices that will spontaneously establish themselves through the free play of the forces of supply and demand.*

2. *Once established they will persist, unless the forces of supply and demand themselves change.*

There is one last thing carefully to be noted about equilibrium prices. *They are the prices that bring about an equality in the quantities demanded and the quantities supplied.* They are not the prices that bring about an equality of "supply and demand." Probably the commonest beginning mistake in economics is to say that supply and demand are equal when prices are in equilibrium. But if we remember that both supply and demand mean the *relationships* between quantities and prices, we can see that this would mean that the demand schedule and the supply schedule for a commodity were alike, so that the curves would lie one on top of the other. In turn, this would mean that at a price of $50, buyers of shoes would be willing and able to buy the same number of shoes that suppliers would be willing to offer at that price, and the same for sellers at $5. If such were the case, prices would be wholly indeterminate and could race high and low with no tension of opposing interests to bring them to a stable resting place.

Hence we must take care to use the words *supply* or *demand* to refer only to relationships or schedules, and to use the longer phrase *quantity demanded* or *quantity supplied* when we want to speak of the effect of a particular price on our willingness or ability either to buy or sell.

The role of competition

We have seen how stable, lasting prices spontaneously emerge from the flux of the marketplace. But we have silently passed over a basic condition for the formation of these prices. This is the role played by competition in the operation of the market mechanism.

How does competition fit into the process of establishing equilibrium prices? The answer is that it provides the regulator that "supervises" the orderly working of the market. It does so because economic competition, unlike the competition for prizes outside economic life, is not a single contest, but a *continuing process* — a race in which the runners never win but must go on endlessly trying to stay in front to avoid the penalties of falling behind.

Second, unlike the contests of ordinary life, economic *competition involves not just a single struggle among rivals, but two struggles,* one of them between the two sides of the markets and the other among the marketers on each side. For the competitive marketplace is not only where the clash of interest between buyer and seller is worked out by the opposition of supply and demand, but also where buyers contend against buyers and sellers against sellers.

It is this double aspect of the competitive process that accounts for its usefulness. A market in which buyers and sellers had no conflict of interest would not be competitive, for prices could then be arranged at some level convenient for both sides, instead of representing a compromise between the divergent interests of the two. And a market that was no more than a place where opposing forces contended would be only a tug of war, a bargaining contest with an outcome about which we could say nothing unless we knew the respective strengths and cunning of the two sides.

It is the fact that each side of the price contest is also contesting against itself—the fact that vying takes place not merely *between* those who want high prices and those who want low ones, but on each side of this divide *among* marketers whose self-interest urges them to meet the demands of the other side—that makes a competition a process that drives buyers and sellers to a meeting point. If some of our unsatisfied shoe buyers, for example—although preferring low prices to high ones—were not pushed into offering a little higher price than the prevailing one by their desire to get shoes, and if some unsatisfied sellers, although hoping for high prices, were not driven by self-interest to offer a price a little below that of their rivals, the price would not move to that balancing point where the two sides arrived at the best possible settlement.

Thus competition is a key condition for the operation of a market system. What are we to make, then, of the fact that we know that monopolistic and oligopolistic elements are to be found in many markets in the real economy? We shall have to wait until Chapter 7 before we can fully analyze the effect that these market imperfections have on the solutions to market problems; but suffice it to say now that for all the departures they will introduce from the competitive model, the basic relevance of that model will still apply. Moreover, until we have understood how a competitive market works, we will not be able to understand the differences that monopoly or oligopoly introduce.

Hence, during the next several chapters we will be proceeding under the assumption of "pure" competition. In due course we will examine very carefully exactly what we mean by this kind of competition and the extent to which economic reasoning built on it is applicable to the real world. But there is a good deal to learn before we add these finishing touches to our microeconomic knowledge.

Prices and allocation

We have already cleared up a good deal of the mystery about how prices are formed in a market system. Although we have not really looked into supply curves (and we cannot until we probe the operations of the firm) we understand in general that prices for most goods on the marketplace reflect the interplay of the demand schedules of consumers and the supply schedules of producers. In our next chapter we will see how changes in demand affect prices and how various characteristics of demand exert different influences on the price structure.

But before we turn to the dynamics of supply and demand, there is a further illumination that our understanding of the price mechanism can shed on the problems of microeconomics. It begins to explain to us how the market system solves the problems of allocation with which it is entrusted. In particular it clears up the puzzle of how the market system *rations* goods among claimants.

In one form or another, rationing—or the allocation of goods among consumers—is a disagreeable but inescapable task that every economic system must carry out; for in all societies, the prevailing reality of life has been the inadequacy of output to fill the needs of the people. In traditional economies, we will remember, rationing is performed by a general adherence to rigidly established rules that determine the rights of various individuals to share in the social product, whether by caste or class or family position or whatever. In command societies, the division of the social product is carried out in a more explicitly directed fashion, as the authorities—lords, priests, kings, commissars—determine the rights of various groups or persons to share in the fruits of society.

A market society, as we know, dispenses with the heavy hand of tradition or the arbitrary one of command, but it too must impose some system of rationing to prevent what would otherwise be an impossibly destructive struggle among its citizens. This critical allocative task is also accomplished by the price mechanism. *For one of the prime functions of a market is to determine who shall be allowed to acquire goods and who shall not.*

Imagine a market in which we have ten buyers, each willing and able to buy one unit of a commodity, but each having a different price that is agreeable to him, and ten suppliers, each also willing and able to put one unit of supply on the market, again each at a different price. Such a market might look like Table 2-3.

As we can see, the equilibrium price will lie at $6, for at this price there will be five suppliers of one unit each and five purchasers of one each. Now let us make a graph in which each bar stands for a single individual, and where the height of the bar tells us how much that individual will be willing to pay for the unit of the commodity or how much

**TABLE
2 • 3**

Price	Number willing and able to buy one unit at this price	Number willing and able to sell one unit at this price
$11	0	10
10	1	9
9	2	8
8	3	7
7	4	6
6	5	5
5	6	4
4	7	3
3	8	2
2	9	1
1	10	0

he would sell it for. If we line up our marketers in order of their demand and supply capabilities, our market will look like Fig. 2-3.

What we have drawn is in fact nothing but a standard supply and demand diagram. But look what it shows us. All the buyers who can afford and are willing to pay the equilibrium price (or more) will get the good they want. All those who cannot, will not. So, too, all the sellers who are willing and able to supply the commodity at its equilibrium price or less will be able to consummate sales. All those who cannot, will not.

Thus the market, in establishing an equilibrium price, has in effect allocated the goods among some buyers and withheld it from others, and permitted some sellers to do business and denied that privilege to others. In our previous case, anyone who could pay $25 or more got a pair of shoes, and all those who could not were unable to get shoes; while all producers who could turn out shoes for $25 or less were able to do

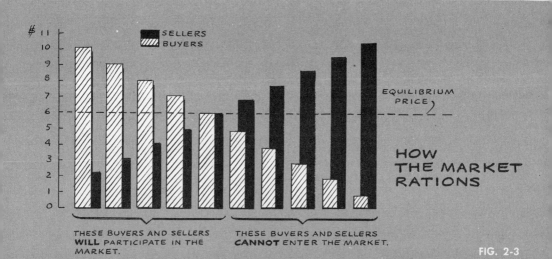

SELLERS
BUYERS

EQUILIBRIUM PRICE

HOW
THE MARKET
RATIONS

THESE BUYERS AND SELLERS **WILL** PARTICIPATE IN THE MARKET.

THESE BUYERS AND SELLERS **CANNOT** ENTER THE MARKET.

FIG. 2-3

business, and those who could not meet that price were unable to make any sales at all.

Note that the market is in this way a means of excluding certain people from economic activity — namely, customers with too little money or with too weak desires, or suppliers unwilling or unable to operate at a certain price.

Price vs. nonprice rationing

The rationing system of the market is both its triumph and its trouble. The complications that arise in nonmarket control mechanisms vary with different economies. In the case of tradition, for instance, the problem is the profound inertia that comes from a static arrangement of economic duties and rewards. In the case of command economies, the problem lies in the difficulty of administering a system without resort to bureaucratic inefficiency on the one hand or dictatorial intervention on the other.

Against these very grave difficulties of other systems, the price system has two great advantages: (1) *it is highly dynamic,* and (2) *it is self-enforcing.* That is, on the one hand it provides an easy avenue for change to enter the system, while on the other, it permits economic activity to take place without anyone "overseeing" the system.

The second (self-regulating) attribute of the market is especially useful with regard to the rationing function. In place of ration tickets with their almost inevitable black markets or cumbersome inspectorates or queues of customers trying to be first in line, *the price system operates without any kind of visible administrative apparatus or side effect.* The energies that must go into planning, or the frictions that come out of it, are alike rendered unnecessary by the self-policing market mechanism.

On the other hand, the system has the defects of its virtues. If it is efficient and dynamic, it is also devoid of values: it recognizes no priorities of claim to the goods and services of society except those of wealth and income. In a society in which all shared alike, or in which incomes were distributed in accordance with some universally approved principle, this neutrality of the market would be perfectly acceptable, for then each would enter the market on equal terms or at least with advantages and disadvantages that bore the stamp of social approval.* But in a

---

*Suppose incomes were distributed absolutely evenly among all families. What would happen to prices? Since tastes are different among different individuals, there would no doubt be a rush to buy some commodities, the prices of which would soar, and a disinclination to buy others, the prices of which would sink. In the end (forgetting about costs for the moment), relative prices would reflect the relative marginal utilities of different goods to the population, and the people who would consume the more expensive goods would be those whose tastes made them willing to spend their money on them.

society in which inheritance still perpetuates large fortunes made in the past, and where unemployment or old age can bring extreme deprivation, the rationing results of the market often affront our sense of dignity.

Therefore every market society interferes to some extent with the "natural" outcome of the price rationing system. In times of emergency, such as war, it issues special permits that take precedence over money and thereby prevent the richer members of society from buying up all the supplies of scarce and valuable items, such as gasoline. In depressed areas, it may distribute basic food or clothing to those who have no money to buy them. And to an ever-increasing extent it uses its taxes and transfer payments to redistribute the ration tickets of money in accordance with the prevailing sense of justice and right.

Shortages and surpluses

Our view of the price system as a rationing mechanism helps to clarify the meaning of two words we often hear as a result of intervention into the market-rationing process: *shortage* and *surplus*.

What do we mean when we say there is a *shortage* of housing for low income groups? The everyday meaning is that people with low incomes cannot find enough housing. Yet in every market there are always some buyers who are unsatisfied. We have just noted, for instance, that in our shoe market, all buyers who could not or would not pay $25 had to go without shoes. Does this mean there was a shoe "shortage"?

Certainly no one uses that word to describe the outcome of a normal market, even though there are always buyers and sellers who are excluded from that market because they cannot meet the going price. Then what does a "shortage" mean? *We can see now that it usually refers to a situation in which the price has been fixed by some nonmarket agency, such as the government, below the equilibrium price.*

Figure 2-4 shows us such a situation. Note that at the price established by the government, the quantity demanded is much greater than the quantity supplied. If this were a free market, the price would soon rise to the equilibrium point, and we would hear no more about a short-

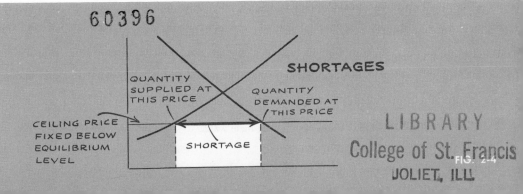

age. But so long as the price is fixed at ceiling level, this equilibrating process cannot take place. Thus the quantity demanded will remain larger than the quantity supplied, and some buyers will go unsatisfied *even though they were willing and able to pay the going price.*

The opposite takes place with a surplus. Here, in Fig. 2-5, we see a price floor fixed above the equilibrium price, as when the government supports crops above their free market price.

Now we have a situation in which the quantity supplied is greater than that demanded (note that we do not say that "supply" is greater than "demand"). In a free market the price would fall until the two quantities were equal. But if the government continues to support the commodity, then more will be produced than the amount for which there will be private buyers. The unsold amounts will be a "surplus."

Thus the words shortage *and* surplus *mean situations in which there are sellers and buyers who are willing and able to enter the market at the going price but who remain active and unsatisfied because the price mechanism has not eliminated them.* This is very different from a free market where there are unsatisfied buyers and sellers *who cannot meet the going price* and who are therefore not taken into account. Poor people have no demand for fresh caviar at $40 per pound and therefore do not complain of a caviar shortage, but if the price of fresh caviar were set by government decree at $1 a pound, there would soon be a colossal "shortage."

What about the situation with low cost housing? Essentially what we mean when we talk of a shortage of inexpensive housing is that we view the outcome of this particular market situation with noneconomic eyes and pronounce the result distasteful. By the standards of the market, the poor who cannot afford to buy housing are simply buyers at the extreme lower right end of the demand curve, and their elimination from the market for housing is only one more example of the rationing process that takes place in *every* market. When we single out certain goods or services (such as doctor's care or higher education) as being in "short supply," we imply that we do not approve of the price mechanism as the appropriate means of allocating scarce resources in these particular instances. This is not because the market is not as efficient a distributor

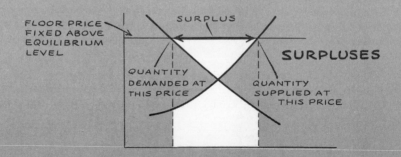

FLOOR PRICE FIXED ABOVE EQUILIBRIUM LEVEL

SURPLUS

SURPLUSES

QUANTITY DEMANDED AT THIS PRICE

QUANTITY SUPPLIED AT THIS PRICE

FIG. 2-5

as ever. It is because in these instances we feel that the underlying distribution (or maldistribution) of income causes the outcome of the market rationing process to clash with other standards of the public interest that we value even more highly than the standard of efficiency.

Summary

1. In the market system, prices give *stimuli* or *signals* telling us how to act to *increase our pecuniary advantage*. Microeconomics is therefore often called *price theory*.
2. *Price stimuli give rise to different economic reactions depending on what side of the market we are located* — that is, whether we are buyers or sellers.
3. The actions of both buyers and sellers reflect both their *willingness* and their *ability* to purchase or sell. Thus the words *demand* and *supply* tell us what *quantities* will be bought and sold *at different prices*.
4. Our willingness to buy larger quantities at lower prices is explained by the hypothesis that the *marginal utility of goods diminishes* as we possess more and more of them (within a fixed period of time).
5. *Demand and supply are both functional relationships* that describe our behavior at different prices.
6. In a competitive market, prices will be determined by the interaction of buyers and sellers. *At low prices the quantities demanded will exceed the quantities supplied, and vice versa at high prices. The prices at which the quantities demanded and supplied are equal is called the equilibrium price.* (Note that "demand" and "supply" are *not* equal at this price.)
7. *At equilibrium prices the market clears.* Because quantities demanded and supplied are identical, there are no unsatisfied buyers or sellers able and willing to enter the market and therefore to alter its quantities offered or sought.
8. Equilibrium prices will *spontaneously establish themselves* in competitive markets and will *persist* until the forces of supply or demand change.
9. Markets depend not only on *self-interest,* but on the force of *competition.* This is the outcome of *two struggles* — one across the market and another on either side of the market.
10. Prices perform an *allocatory function, rationing goods* among those buyers and sellers who are willing and able to enter the market at the going price. This rationing system is *highly dynamic* and is *self-enforcing.* At the same time, it recognizes no distributive principles or values except those of wealth.
11. *Shortages and surpluses* refer to situations in which prices have been imposed on a market and are below or above the equilibrium price. We do not count as victims of shortage or surplus the unsatisfied buyers or sellers we encounter in an equilibrium market. When we do label a situation as "shortage" or "surplus," it means that we do not approve of the market system as an appropriate rationing device for that good or service.

Questions

1. Why is microeconomics called price theory? What different things does the same price signal mean to buyers and sellers? Do sellers and buyers, for example, both like falling prices?

2. What is meant by saying that demand is a function of price? Does this mean that we will buy more of a good when its prices go up? What are the motivational roots of "demand"? Why is not our ability to buy—our income—enough to give us a demand schedule?

3. Why would the marginal utility of bread and diamonds change if you were locked in Tiffany's over the week end? Why are so many necessities of life so inexpensive, when they are indispensable?

4. Draw up a hypothetical demand schedule for yourself for one year's purchases of books, assuming that the average price of books changed from $10 through $1.

5. Draw up a supply schedule for your local bookstore, assuming that book prices ranged from $1 to $10.

6. What is the equilibrium price of books in your examples above? Exactly what do you mean by equilibrium price? What is special about the quantities demanded and supplied at this price?

7. What is the difference between "supply and demand" and "quantity supplied" and "quantity demanded"?

8. What do we mean when we say that there are two aspects to competition? What are they? Why is any one not enough?

9. What is meant by allocation? How do prices allocate goods among buyers?

10. What is meant by a surplus? A shortage? Draw diagrams to illustrate each.

11. A British critic of their National Health Service has written: "If taxi fares and meters were abolished and a free National Taxi service were financed by taxation, who would go by car or bus, or walk? . . . The shortage of taxis would be endemic, rationing by rushing would go to the physically strong, and be more arbitrary than price, and the 'taxi crisis' a subject of periodic agitation and political debate." Discuss this statement in view of what you know about the rationing mechanism. What light does it throw on the "shortage" of doctors in England today? Assuming that the argument is valid in its charge that taxi rationing by rushing would be more arbitrary than by price, does it follow that medical rationing by price is the least arbitrary system?

3

The market in movement

We have learned how equilibrium prices emerge "mysteriously and marvellously" from the wholly unsupervised interaction of competing buyers and sellers; and we have seen how those prices, once formed, silently and efficiently perform the necessary social task of allocating goods among buyers and sellers. Yet our analysis is still too static to resemble the actual play of the marketplace. For one of the attributes of an equilibrium price, we remember, is its lasting quality, its persistence. But the prices around us in the real world are often in movement. How can we introduce this element of change into our analysis of microeconomic relations?

The answer is that the word *equilibrium* in micro analysis no more implies changelessness than it does in macro analysis. Equilibrium prices are indeed lasting — so long as the forces that produce them do not change, but just as shifts in saving and investment continuously reset the point of equilibrium for GNP, so changes in supply and demand constantly alter the resting point of individual prices.

But what makes supply and demand change? If we recall the definition of those words, we are asking *what might change our willingness or ability to buy or sell something at any given price?* The basic reasons are not difficult to discover. Suppose, for instance, that in the course of our previous adventure in shirt buying, we had taken out our wallet and found that we had less money in it than we imagined. Such a change in our financial circumstances would be very likely to alter the quantity of merchandise we were willing and able to acquire. The discovery of additional money would also affect our demand — but in the opposite direction.

A similar change in financial circumstances would also alter the willingness and ability of the supplier to make various quantities

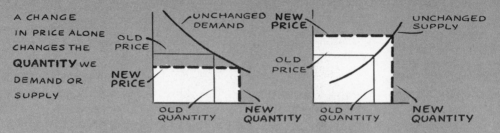

FIG. 3-1

CHANGES IN QUANTITIES DEMANDED OR SUPPLIED

of shirts at various prices. If the cost of shirt material fell sharply, our tailor might be perfectly willing and able to make shirts at $4.50 (whereas formerly he could not afford to); and might find it profitable to make a larger quantity of shirts than he did previously at higher prices.

Psychological changes in our condition as buyers or sellers can alter our willingness and ability to buy or sell equally as much as financial changes. A change in our tastes, induced by advertising or whatever, can make us more or less willing to spend our money for a given commodity, even though its price remains the same. A change in our attitudes toward work may make us more or less willing to undertake a given job at a given price: our tailor may decide to give up tailoring altogether or to make his fame as a designer of shirts. Either would change the quantity of shirts he would produce at various prices.

Thus changes in taste or attitudes, or in income or wealth will shift our whole demand schedule, and the same changes, plus any change in costs, will shift our whole supply schedule. Note that this is very different from a change in the quantity we buy or sell when *prices* change. In the first case, as our willingness and ability to buy or sell is increased or diminished, *the whole demand and supply schedule (or curve) shifts bodily.* In the second place, when our basic willingness and ability is unchanged, but prices change, our schedule (or curve) is unchanged, but *we move back or forth along it.*

Here are the two cases to be studied carefully in Fig. 3-1. Note that when our demand schedule shifts, we will buy a *different amount at the same price.* If our willingness and ability to buy is enhanced, we will buy a larger amount; if they are diminished, a smaller amount. Similarly, the quantity a seller will offer will vary as his willingness and ability are altered. Thus demand and supply curves can shift about, rightward and leftward, up and down, as the economic circumstances they represent change. In reality, these schedules are continuously in change, since tastes and incomes and attitudes and technical capabilities (which affect costs and therefore sellers' actions) are also continuously in flux.

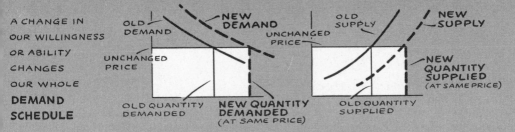

A CHANGE IN
OUR WILLINGNESS
OR ABILITY
CHANGES
OUR WHOLE
**DEMAND
SCHEDULE**

vs. CHANGES IN DEMAND OR SUPPLY

FIG. 3-1 (Cont.)

Price changes

How do changes in supply and demand affect prices? We have already seen the underlying process at work in the case of shoes. Changes in supply or demand will alter the *quantities* that will be sought or offered on the market at a given price—an increase in demand, for instance, will raise the quantity sought. Since there are not enough goods offered to match this quantity, price will be bid up by unsatisfied buyers to a new level at which quantities offered and sought again balance. Similarly, if supply shifts, there will be too much or too little put on the market in relation to the existing quantity of demand, and competition among sellers will push prices up or down to a new level at which quantities sought and offered again clear.

In Fig. 3-2, we show what happens to the equilibrium price in two cases—first, when demand increases (perhaps due to a sudden craze for the good in question); second, when demand decreases (when the craze is over). Quite obviously, a rise in demand—other things being equal—will cause prices to rise, and a fall in demand will cause them to fall.

We can depict the same process from the supply side. In Fig. 3-3, we show the impact on price of a sudden rise in supply and of a fall. Again the diagram makes clear what is intuitively obvious: an increased supply (given an unchanging demand) leads to lower prices; a decreased supply to higher prices.

And if supply and demand *both* change? Then the result will be higher or lower prices, depending on the shapes and new positions of the two

CHANGES IN EQUILIBRIUM PRICES DUE TO SHIFTS IN DEMAND

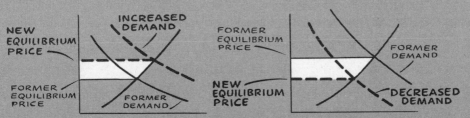

FIG. 3-2

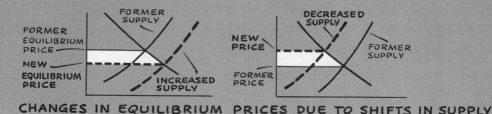

FORMER EQUILIBRIUM PRICE

NEW EQUILIBRIUM PRICE

FORMER SUPPLY

INCREASED SUPPLY

DECREASED SUPPLY

NEW PRICE

FORMER SUPPLY

FORMER PRICE

CHANGES IN EQUILIBRIUM PRICES DUE TO SHIFTS IN SUPPLY

FIG. 3-3

curves—that is, depending on the relative changes in the willingness and ability of both sides. Figure 3-4 shows a few possibilities.

Elasticities

Out of these various possibilities, how do we know which will occur? Suppose that demand schedules have increased, say by 10 per cent. Do we know how much of an effect this change will have on price?

These questions lead us to a still deeper scrutiny of the nature of supply and demand, by way of a new concept called *elasticity* or, more properly, *price elasticity*. Elasticities describe the shapes of supply and demand curves, and thereby tell us a good deal as to whether a given change in demand or supply will have a small or large effect on price.

Figure 3-5 illustrates the case with two supply curves. Our diagrams show two commodities selling at the same equilibrium prices and facing identical demand schedules. Note, however, that the two commodities have very different supply curves. In both cases demand now increases by the same amount. Notice how much greater is the price increase in the case of the good with the inelastic supply curve.

Similarly, the price change that would be associated with a change in supply will be greater for a commodity with an inelastic demand curve than for one with an elastic demand curve. Figure 3-6 shows two identical supply curves matched against very different demand curves.

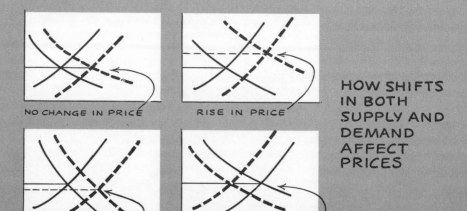

NO CHANGE IN PRICE

RISE IN PRICE

FALL IN PRICE

NO CHANGE IN PRICE

HOW SHIFTS IN BOTH SUPPLY AND DEMAND AFFECT PRICES

FIG. 3-4

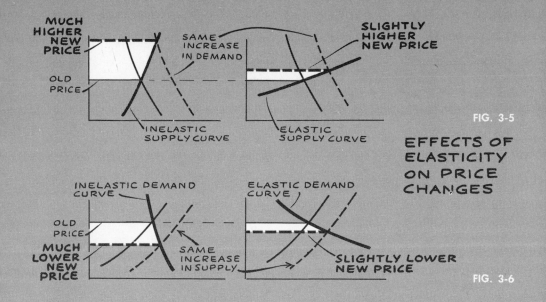

FIG. 3-5

EFFECTS OF
ELASTICITY
ON PRICE
CHANGES

FIG. 3-6

Note how much greater is the fall in price of the commodity for which demand is inelastic.

Clearly, elasticities are powerful factors in explaining price movements.* This is because the word "elasticity" refers to our sensitivity of response to price changes. What we mean by an elastic demand (or supply) is that, as buyers or sellers, our willingness or ability to buy or sell is strongly affected by changes in price, whereas when our schedules are inelastic, the effect is small. In more precise terms, *an elastic demand (or supply) is one in which a given percentage change in prices brings about a larger percentage change in the quantity demanded (or supplied)*. An inelastic schedule or curve is one in which the response in the quantities we are willing and able to buy or sell is proportionally less than the change in price.†

It helps if we see what elasticities of different kinds look like. Figure

---

*We should notice that we can use another term—*income elasticity*—to describe the response of our willingness and ability to buy and sell, not to a change in price, but to a change in our incomes. There are some goods—cigarettes are evidently one—in which the quantities we buy seem to be more influenced by changes in income than by normal fluctuations in price. For other goods, such as coffee, it has been estimated that housewives' purchases are more influenced by changes in price than by fluctuations in income. In the real world, price and income elasticities are inextricably mixed, but we will confine our attention here to the simpler case of price elasticity alone.

† Notice that elasticity is a *quantitative* notion—that it is measured by changes in quantities bought or sold compared with changes in price. This caution is needed because it is possible to make demand or supply curves "look" elastic or inelastic by changing the calibration of the horizontal or vertical axes on a diagram. For simplicity's sake we will continue to rely on the visual "look" of elasticity and inelasticity, but the student should remember that the real test is provided by the proportional changes in quantities, not by the possibly misleading shapes he sees.

1. TOTALLY INELASTIC DEMAND OR SUPPLY. The quantity offered or sought is unchanged despite a change in price. Examples: Within normal price ranges there is probably no change at all in the quantity of table salt bought. Similarly, a fisherman landing a catch of fish will have to sell it all at any price—within reason.

2. INELASTIC DEMAND OR SUPPLY. The quantity offered or sought changes proportionately less than the price. Examples: We probably do not double our bread purchases if the price of bread halves. On the supply side, the price of wheat may double, but farmers are unable (at least for a long while) to offer twice as much wheat for sale.

3. UNIT ELASTICITY. This is a special case in which quantities demanded or supplied respond in exact proportion to price changes. (Note the shape of the demand curve.) Examples: Many goods may fit this description, but it is impossible flatly to state that any one good does so.

4. ELASTIC DEMAND OR SUPPLY. Price changes induce proportionally larger changes in quantity. Examples: Many luxury goods increase dramatically in sales volume when their price is lowered. On the supply side, elastic demand usually affects items that are easy to produce, so that a small price rise induces a rush for expanded output.

5. TOTALLY ELASTIC DEMAND OR SUPPLY. The quantity supplied or demanded at the going price is "infinite." Examples: This seemingly odd case turns out to be of great importance in describing the market outlook of the typical small competitive firm. Merely as a hint: for an individual farmer, the demand curve for

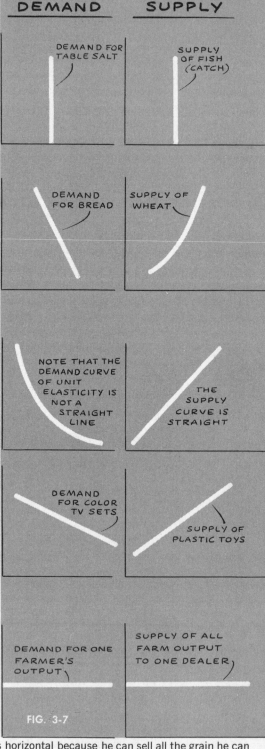

DEMAND SUPPLY

DEMAND FOR TABLE SALT

SUPPLY OF FISH (CATCH)

DEMAND FOR BREAD

SUPPLY OF WHEAT

NOTE THAT THE DEMAND CURVE OF UNIT ELASTICITY IS NOT A STRAIGHT LINE

THE SUPPLY CURVE IS STRAIGHT

DEMAND FOR COLOR TV SETS

SUPPLY OF PLASTIC TOYS

DEMAND FOR ONE FARMER'S OUTPUT

SUPPLY OF ALL FARM OUTPUT TO ONE DEALER

FIG. 3-7

his output at the going price looks horizontal because he can sell all the grain he can possibly raise at that price. A grain dealer can also buy all he wants at that price.

3-7 is a family of supply and demand curves that illustrates the range of buying and selling responses associated with a change in prices.

Elasticities, expenditures, and receipts

Elasticities not only affect the determination of market prices, they also have a very great effect on the fortunes of buyers and sellers in the marketplace. That is, it makes a great deal of difference to a buyer whether the supply curve of a commodity he wants is elastic or not, for that will affect very drastically the amount he will have to spend on that particular commodity if its price changes; and it makes an equal amount of difference to a seller whether the demand curve for his output is elastic or not, for that will determine what happens to his total revenues as prices change.

Here is an instance in point. Table 3-1 shows three demand schedules: elastic, inelastic, and of unit elasticity. Let us see how these three differently shaped schedules would affect the fortunes of a seller who had to cater to the demand represented by each.

TABLE 3 • 1 DEMAND SCHEDULES FOR THREE GOODS (QUANTITIES DEMANDED)

Price	Inelastic demand	Unit elasticity	Elastic demand
10	100	100	100
9	101	111 1/9	120
8	102	125	150
7	103	143	200
6	104	166 2/5	300
5	105	200	450
4	106	250	650
3	107	333 1/3	900
2	108	500	1,400
1	109	1,000	3,000

Now a very interesting result follows from these different schedules. *The total amount spent for each commodity (and thus the total amount received by a firm) will be very different over the indicated range of prices.* In Table 3-2 are the amounts spent (price times quantity).

We can see that it makes a lot of difference to a seller whether he is supplying goods for which the demand is elastic or not. *If demand is elastic and he cuts his price, he will take in more revenue.* If his demand is inelastic and he cuts his price, he will take in *less* revenue. (This has typically been the case with farm products, as we recall from our history.)

Conversely, a businessman who raises his price will be lucky if the demand for his product is inelastic, for then his receipts will actually

TABLE   TOTAL EXPENDITURES (OR RECEIPTS)
3 • 2

Price	Good with inelastic demand	Good with unit elasticity demand	Good with elastic demand
10	1,000	1,000	1,000
9	909	1,000	1,080
8	816	1,000	1,200
7	717	1,000	1,400
6	612	1,000	1,800
5	525	1,000	2,250
4	424	1,000	2,600
3	321	1,000	2,700
2	216	1,000	2,800
1	109	1,000	3,000

increase. Compare the fortunes of the two businessmen as depicted in Fig. 3-8. Note that by blocking in the change in price times the change in quantity, we can show the change in receipts. (Because we have ignored changes in costs, we cannot show changes in profits.)

Obviously, what every businessman would like to have is a demand for his product that was inelastic in an upward direction and elastic at lower than existing prices, so that he stood to gain whether he raised or lowered prices. As we shall see when we study pricing under oligopoly, just the opposite is apt to be the case.

Behind elasticities of demand

Because elasticities are so important in accounting for the behavior of prices, we must press our investigation further. However, we must leave the supply side of elasticity to be studied in our next chapter when we look into the behavior of factors and for later chapters when we will study the operation of firms. Here we will ask why are demand curves

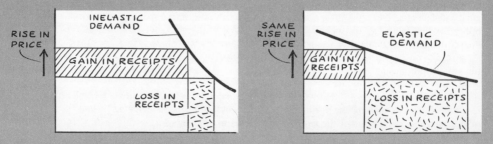

HOW ELASTICITIES AFFECT RECEIPTS WHEN PRICES CHANGE

FIG. 3-8

shaped the way they are? Why is our price (or income) sensitivity for some commodities so great and for others so slight?

If we think of a good or service for which our demand might be very inelastic — say eyeglasses (assuming we need them) — and compare it with another for which our demand is apt to be highly elastic — say, a trip to Europe — the difference is not difficult to grasp. One thing is a necessity; the other is a luxury. But what do we mean by *necessity* and *luxury?* If we think more carefully about the terms, we can define them still more clearly in terms of the ease with which we can *substitute* other goods or services in their place.

A necessity is a good for which it is hard to find substitutes. If we need eyeglasses, we will spend a great deal of money, if need be, to acquire a pair. Hence such a necessity has a very inelastic demand curve.*

That is easy to see as prices rise. But what about when they fall? Won't we rush to buy necessities, just because they *are* necessities? Won't that make their demand curves elastic?

Surprisingly, the answer is that we do not rush to buy necessities when their prices fall. Why? The answer is that necessities are the things we buy *first,* just because they are necessities. Having bought what we needed before the fall in price, we are not tempted to buy much more, if any more, after the fall. Bread, as we commented before, is a great deal more valuable for life than diamonds are, but we ordinarily have enough bread, so that the marginal utility of another loaf is no greater than that of an equivalent expenditure on any other good. Thus, as the price of bread drops, the quantity we seek expands only slightly. So, too, with eyeglasses.

Compare the case with a luxury, such as a trip to Europe. There are many substitutes for such a trip — trips out West, trips South, or some

---

*Necessities are never absolute in the sense that nothing can be substituted for the commodity in question. High enough prices will drive buyers to *some* substitute, however imperfect. Just when will the buyer be driven to the next-best-thing? Traditionally, economists describe the decision as determined by a comparison of the marginal utility derived from a dollar's worth of the high-priced item with that derived from the lower-priced substitute. As the price of champagne goes up and up, there comes a point when we would rather spend our next dollar for a substantial amount of beer, rather than for a sip of champagne.

We can describe *all* consumer purchasing as following this pattern of maximizing marginal satisfactions. Presumably we always buy the thing that gives us the highest marginal utility for the dollar we are spending at any particular moment. As we buy more of the "best" thing, its marginal utility to us diminishes, and we buy the next most satisfying thing. As a result, we end up with a situation in which the marginal utility of a dollar spent by us for *any* good brings in the same amount of satisfaction. We say "presumably," since marginal utility cannot actually be measured. A number of economists have correctly pointed out that there can be no *proof* that we equalize marginal utilities by our actions. Nonetheless, the concept of maximizing our marginal utilities by "comparison shopping" seems to offer a plausible description of the motives that guide us as buyers.

other kind of vacation. As a result, if the price of a European trip goes up, we are easily persuaded to switch to some alternative plan. Conversely, when the price of a European trip gets cheaper. we are quick to substitute *it* for other possible vacation alternatives and our demand accordingly displays its elastic properties.

Do not make the mistake, however, of thinking that elasticity is purely a function of whether items are "expensive" or not. Studies have shown that the demand for subway transportation in New York City is price-elastic, which hardly means that riding in the subway is the prerogative of millionaires. The point, rather, is that the demand for subway rides is closely affected by the comparative prices of substitutes—bus fares and taxis. Thus *it is the ease or difficulty of substitution that always lies behind the various elasticities of demand schedules.*

The importance of time

Time also plays an important role in shaping our demand curves. Suppose, for example, that the price of orange juice suddenly soared, owing to a crop failure. Would the demand for orange juice be elastic or inelastic?

In the short run, it would certainly be more inelastic than in the longer run. Lovers of orange juice would likely be willing to pay a higher price for their favorite juice because (they would believe) there was really no other juice quite as good. But as the weeks went by they might be tempted to try other breakfast juices, and no doubt some of these experiments would "take." Substitutes would be found, after all.

The point is that it takes time and information for patterns of demand to change. Thus demand curves become more elastic as time goes on, and the range of discovered substitutes becomes larger.

Substitution and demand

There is a last point we should make before we leave the subject of substitution. We have seen that the substitutability of one product for another is the underlying cause of elasticity. Indeed, more and more we are led to see "products" themselves as bundles of utilities surrounded with other competing bundles that offer a whole range of alternatives for a buyer's satisfaction.

What is it that ultimately determines how close the substitutes come to the commodity in question? As with all questions in economics that are pursued to the end, the answer lies in two aspects of reality before which economic inquiry comes to a halt. One of these is the human being himself, with his tastes and drives and wants. One man's substitute will not be another's.

The other ultimate basing point for economics is the technical and physical nature of the world that forces certain relationships of ends and means upon us. Cotton may be a substitute for wool because they both have the properties of fibers, but diamonds are not a substitute for the same end-use because they lack the requisite physical properties. Diamonds, as finery, may be a substitute for clothes made out of cotton, but until we learn how to spin diamonds, they will not be a substitute for the cloth itself.

Because substitutes form a vast chain of alternatives for buyers, changes in the prices of substitutes change the positions of demand curves. Here is a new idea to be thought about carefully. Our existing demand curve for bread or diamonds has the shape (elasticity) it does because substitutes exist at various prices. But when the prices of those substitutes *change*, the original commodity suddenly looks "cheaper" or "more expensive." If the price of subway rides rises from 20 cents to 25 cents, while the price of taxi rides remains the same, we will be tempted to switch part of our transportation from subways to taxis. If subway rides went to 50 cents, there would be a mass exodus to taxis. Thus we should add changes in the prices of substitutes to changes in taste and in income when we consider the possible causes of a shift in demand. If the price of a substitute commodity rises, the demand for the original commodity will rise; and as the price of substitutes falls, demand for the original commodity will fall.

Complements

There is another connection between commodities beside that of substitution—the relationship of *complementarity*. Complementarity means that some commodities are technically linked, so that you cannot very well use one without using the other, even though they are sold separately. Automobiles and gasoline are examples of such complementary goods, as are cameras and film.

Here is another instance in which changes in the price of one good actually affect the position of the demand curve for the other. If the price of film goes up, it becomes more expensive to operate cameras. Hence the demand for cameras is apt to drop. Note that the price of cameras has not changed. Rather, when the price of the complementary good—the film—goes up, the whole demand curve for cameras shifts to the left.

Individual and collective demand, again

We are almost ready to take our first overview of the whole market system, but there is still a missing link in our analysis chain. We have dealt thus far largely in terms of individual demand and supply schedules and curves—that is, in terms of the motivation between one person's willingness and ability to buy or sell. In a macroeconomic study, however, we would speak of demand and supply in collective or sectorial or national terms. How do we connect the two?

When we speak of the national demand for, or supply of, a good or service, we are really doing no more than adding up all the demand schedules of the individuals concerned. Thus the national demand for automobiles is a schedule whose shape and position reflects the sum of the tastes, incomes, preferences, etc., of all persons willing and able to buy cars.

The situation is more complicated, however, when we speak of demand on a still larger scale—for instance, the demand for all consumption goods, or the demand for GNP itself. Some of the relationships we have discovered in this chapter continue to hold. We have already spoken of the effect of a change in income on total consumption demand when we discussed the propensity to consume schedule. We can now see this schedule as a demand curve that relates our willingness and ability to buy all consumption goods at different levels of aggregate income. On the other hand, some attributes of demand at the micro level disappear when we magnify them to macro size. For example, problems of changing tastes, or of substitutes and complements, are usually unimportant in analyzing macroeconomic phenomena, for they represent shifts *within* the sphere of consumption and do not affect the *total* of consumption spending.

More complex is the matter of price and total spending. Can we speak of a price elasticity of total consumption demand? Will consumption spending fall, as a percentage of disposable personal income, if all prices rise? The trouble in answering this question from the perspective of microeconomics is that we have to balance two contradictory effects. Higher prices throughout the economy will mean higher incomes for some people and therefore increased consumer demand. For others however, higher prices will bear against fixed incomes and may well cause a contraction in total expenditures. (Then, just to complicate matters further, higher prices will mean both higher revenues and higher costs to producers, thereby involving us in the supply side of the situation.)

It is easier to deal with questions such as this by going over to the macroeconomic perspective and coping directly with statistical aggregates, such as the marginal propensity to consume, than by trying to calculate the positive income elasticities of millions of consumers against the negative price elasticities of others. Nonetheless, the illustration reminds us that the macro effects we deal with are made up, in fact, of innumerable small micro reactions which constitute the fundamental source of all private economic activity.

The market as a self-correcting mechanism

We have begun to see how the market for goods and services operates as a dynamic, constantly altering—and yet self-adjusting—mechanism. From the interplay of supply and demand schedules for goods emerge equilibrium prices of those goods. Yet these prices are rarely at rest. As the incomes and tastes of the throngs of goods-seekers change—or as the conditions of supply change—the prices of goods are continuously seeking new levels that will equate, if only for a moment, the quantities offered and sought. Moreover, as the prices of goods change, new ripples of disturbance are set into motion, for each good is a substitute for (or perhaps a complement of) others, and thus as each price changes, it will induce shifts in the demand curves that affect other prices. Meanwhile, the ever-shifting pattern of prices is silently carrying out its task of allocating the products on the market among the throng seeking them, distributing goods and permitting sales to those who meet the test of going prices, and quietly but uncompromisingly refusing them to those who do not.

How is order maintained in this extraordinary flux of activity? We have learned a good deal about some of the basic principles that keep the process smoothly and continuously working. One of these, we have seen, is the pressure of self-interest that drives buyer and seller to seek their respective economic advantages—the buyer searching for the cheapest market for the good or service he wants, the seller looking for the highest price for the commodity he wants to sell. The other is the continuous pressure of competition that serves to bring buyer and seller together at a point acceptable to both.

Do self-interest and competition alone guarantee the orderly working of the market? As we shall see, they do not. But to understand why not, we must investigate what we mean by an "orderly" market, in the first place.

Stability and instability

We have already seen one meaning for the word *orderly* in the extraordinary ability of a market situation to produce equilibrium prices

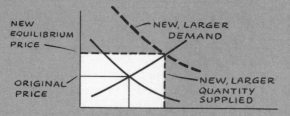

NEW EQUILIBRIUM PRICE

NEW, LARGER DEMAND

ORIGINAL PRICE

NEW, LARGER QUANTITY SUPPLIED

SHORT-RUN CHANGE IN EQUILIBRIUM PRICE

FIG. 3-9

that serve to bring together buyers and sellers in a stable situation of exchange, despite the different directions in which their self-interests propel them.

But we cannot confine orderliness to such a static solution. What happens when things change? Suppose, for example, that the demand curve for shoes shifts because the number of people in town has increased. The first effect of this, we know, will be a new, higher equilibrium price for shoes, as Fig. 3-9 shows. Notice also that at the new higher price, the quantity of shoes supplied will also be larger than it was before.

For the short run, this provides an orderly solution to the problem of change. There is now a new level of prices as stable as before, and a new equally stable level of output. (To be sure, there have been shifts in patterns of spending and in incomes which may exert pressures elsewhere on the economy, but we will ignore that for the moment. As far as the market for shoes is concerned, the problem of change has been met in an orderly way.)

In the long run, however, the process of adjustment is apt to be more complicated.* At higher shoe prices, entrepreneurs in other lines are apt to move into the industry, with the result that the whole supply curve of shoes shifts to the right. As a result, shoe prices will again fall (although we cannot tell by how much unless we know more about the costs of the industry). This solution would look like Fig. 3-10.

Here are two orderly outcomes to a disturbing change. What would be workable outcomes for a *fall* in demand? In the simplest short-run case, a new lower price and a smaller output. A longer-run solution might

*The "long run" is not just a vague figure of speech. It means, in cases like this, the time necessary for producers to build new plant and equipment. Conversely, in the "short run," producers are limited to adjusting their supplies as best as they can from their given plant and equipment.

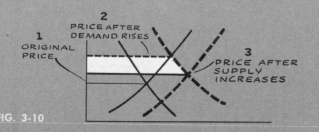

entail an exodus of suppliers and of capital equipment from the industry, so that the supply curve moved leftward and prices again recovered from their initial drop. Whichever the solution, *in the end we would again have stable prices and outputs.*

Unstable situations

Now look at a less reassuring case. This time let us suppose that it takes a considerable time before a larger or smaller demand for a product can be met by a larger or smaller output. Since it takes many months between planting and harvesting, we will choose Christmas trees as the commodity to illustrate this situation for us.

In Fig. 3-11, we show the supply and demand curves for Christmas trees and imagine that the quantity supplied is initially indicated by point *A* on the supply schedule.

We can see that quantity *A* will sell at price *B*. Figuring that this will be next year's price, tree growers now plant the amount they are willing and able to offer at price *B* – quantity *C*. Alas, when the harvest comes, it is found that quantity *C* will fetch only price *D*. Now the process goes into reverse. Growers will figure that next year's price will be *D,* and they plant amount *A*, since at price *D* the quantity they wish to supply is no more than that. Thereupon, next harvest time, the price goes back to *B* – and around we go. If the supply and demand schedules were differently sloped, we *could* have a so-called cobweb that converged toward equilibrium as we show on the left of Fig. 3-12; and we could also have one that "exploded" – as we can see on the right.

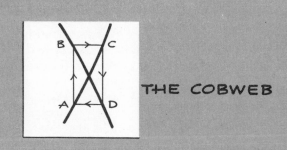

THE COBWEB

FIG. 3-11

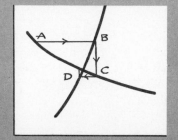
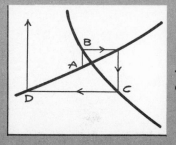

STABILIZING
AND EXPLOSIVE
COBWEBS

FIG. 3-12

Cobwebs show us that markets need not necessarily produce equilib-rium prices. Why, then, do most markets tend toward a resting point and not gyrate or explode like our examples? The answer is that, unlike the cobweb assumptions, most changes in supply are *gradual* and *continu-ous,* so that prices steadily fall as supplies augment, or rise as they dwindle, thus guiding buyer and seller to the appropriate adjustments.

Destabilizing expectations

Cobwebs are something of an anomaly in the market, although they illustrate an important point. But there is another cause of instability that is far from a rarity in the market process. This is the potentially disturb-ing effect of changes in *expectations* on prices and outputs.

We have already encountered expectations as a central agency of economic change when we looked into the motives behind business investment. But investment, for an ordinary business firm, is not an activity undertaken daily. Hence expectations play their role only when a decision must be made whether to expand operations or not.

Not so, in the marketplace. There expectations affect the decisions of marketers virtually every time a purchase or sale is contemplated. More than that, *as expectations change, the motive of self-interest will drive buyers and sellers in directions that imperil the orderly adjustment of the market process.*

To understand this very important point, you must put yourself in the shoes of a buyer or seller who suddenly faces a change—let us say a fall—in prices. What must *you* do to make the market react to that fall in an orderly way, by reaching a new stable equilibrium price?

The answer is that you must behave as our now familiar diagrams say you will behave. As a buyer, you must respond to the fall in price, by buying a larger quantity. As a seller, you must respond by offering somewhat less to the market. In this way, a new stable point of rest will be reached, either further down the demand curve, or—if some suppliers leave the field after a time—perhaps at a higher price along a new supply curve.

But what will make you behave this way? The answer is that your self-interest will, *if you expect that the price fall will go no further or eventually turn around.* Then as a buyer, it will pay you to take advan-tage of lower prices, and as a seller it will cut your losses if you now offer less for sale.

Now suppose, however—and here is the case to be thought about carefully—*that you expect prices to keep on falling.* Then what will your self-interest guide you to do? As a buyer, you will *not* buy more, be-cause you figure, quite correctly, that if you hold off, you will get things still cheaper tomorrow. So too, as a seller, you will *not* offer less, because you fear that if you do not sell as much as you can immediately, you will get even worse prices tomorrow. Thus, in place of the stabilizing reactions that bring a halt to price changes or that may even initiate price reversals, *when expectations themselves are based on runaway price changes, they bring about behavior that creates the very situation they fear.* For in these cases, as buyers hold back and sellers rush forward, the imbalance between quantities supplied and demanded will worsen, and prices will fall further.

The same expectational problem can upset a situation with rising prices. Again, an orderly market requires that the price rise be limited or in time turned around. This requires buyers to demand smaller quantities and sellers to offer larger ones. Both will do exactly that if they anticipate that prices will not rise further. But if expectations become "destabilizing," buyers will react to rising prices by *increasing* the quantities they demand, in order to get them at a better price today than tomorrow; and sellers will hold *back their* supplies, hoping to sell them at higher levels tomorrow. As a result, quantities demanded will increase and supplies offered will fall, and the price rise will accelerate rather than come to a halt.

Predictive and normative price theory

How are such instabilities handled? What effect do they have on the market? In the nature of things, usually they are short-lived affairs that result in wild splurges and busts that disrupt particular markets but do not derange the system as a whole. Sometimes, though, destabilizing reactions can become generalized throughout the whole goods market, as they do when buyers and sellers generally expect an inflation or a depression, and proceed to rush in or hold back in a way that aggravates the very thing they dread. In these cases, destabilizing reactions can be of the gravest importance and must be countered by public policies or public pronouncements aimed at changing peoples' anticipations of the future, so that self-interest will again move them in the direction that brings order rather than disorder.

The narrow line that separates order from disorder, and stability from instability, brings us at the end of this chapter to a final perspective on the subject we are studying. This is the relation of microtheory to the reality of the markets and market behavior in the real world.

Most of us study microtheory in the expectation that it will describe the way markets really are, and therefore serve us in a *predictive* way. And so it will, in a great many cases. When Macy's wants to increase its sales, it lowers its prices in the confident expectation that microeconomics is right when it says that the quantity demanded at lower prices is greater than that at higher ones. Microtheory does describe actual behavior in all "ordinary" cases, and we can and do predict successfully according to its logic.

But sometimes — and these times may be very important — the market does not behave in the way that microtheory describes as the normal case. As we have just seen, this is when expectations turn the normal price-quantity relationships upside down. Yet even in these cases, microeconomics has a special relevance. For it then tells us what behavior would restore normality, and therefore serves as our guidebook when we seek to bring that behavior about. When it is used in this way, price theory is goal-oriented rather than predictive; that is, it tells us how to achieve a desired state of affairs, rather than what will be the outcome of the existing state, left to itself. Both uses are important, one for understanding how the market system is ordinarily capable of producing an orderly solution to the tasks it performs despite the incredibly complicated stimuli that beat upon it; the other for giving us the necessary knowledge to reintroduce order into the system when, under the influence of wild expectations, it threatens to break down.*

Summary

1. Equilibrium prices change when *supply or demand schedules change.* In turn these schedules change when our willingness or ability to buy or sell is altered.
2. *Changes in taste or income* lie behind shifts in demand schedules; behind changes in supply lie *changes in attitudes or costs.*
3. A change in demand (or supply) means a shift of the whole *schedule.* This must be contrasted with changes in the *quantity demanded* (or supplied) which refers to movements *along given curves.*
4. Shifts in demand or supply mean that *different quantities* will be sought or offered *at the same price.*
5. Price elasticities measure the proportionate change in quantities offered or sought when prices change. *Elastic demand* (or supply) means that the *per centage change in quantities demanded* (or supplied) *will be larger than the percentage change in price;* inelastic demand (or supply) means that the percentage quantity change is smaller than the percentage price change.
6. Price elasticities very greatly affect price changes. Price changes will be larger when demand and supply curves are inelastic than when they are elastic. *Elasticities also affect the receipts of the seller or the expenditures of the buyer.*
7. Elasticities reflect the ease or difficulty of *substitution.* Hence, elasticities typically increase over time, as new substitutes are found or as information about them spreads.

*For the fullest discussion of these problems, see Adolph Lowe, *On Economic Knowledge* (Harper & Row, 1965).

8. The *ease of substitution* is an important concept that helps us define what a "*commodity*" is.

9. *Complements* are commodities that are technically linked to one another. The demand for one of them therefore raises or falls with the demand for the other.

10. The market is ordinarily a self-correcting and orderly mechanism. By "*orderly*" *we mean that changes in supply or demand produce new, stable prices and outputs.*

11. In some instances, the outcome of the market is not orderly. One of these is the cobweb situation, where the reaction of supply to demand is not continuous. More important is the case *when expectations are not "stabilizing."*

12. Orderly markets depend on buyers responding to price falls by buying more, and on sellers responding to price falls by offering less. *When either side expects the price fall to continue, these orderly reactions will not be forthcoming.* The result can be a runaway price situation. (The same effect can occur when price rises are not met by the orderly behavior of decreased buying and increased offering.)

13. Microtheory has two uses. It *predicts* the outcome of market situations when behavior is orderly and normal. When behavior is not orderly, it informs us as to *what kind of behavior is needed to restore stability and order to the market.*

Questions

1. What changes in your economic condition would increase your demand for clothes? Draw a diagram to illustrate such a change. Show on it whether you would buy more or less clothes at the prices you formerly paid. If you wanted to buy the same quantity as before, would you be willing and able to pay prices different from those you paid earlier?

2. Suppose that you are a seller of costume jewelry. What changes in your economic condition would decrease your supply curve? Suppose that costs dropped. If demand were unchanged, what would happen to the price in a competitive market?

3. Draw the following: an elastic demand curve and an inelastic supply curve; an inelastic demand curve and an elastic supply curve; a demand curve of infinite elasticity and a totally inelastic supply curve. Now give examples of commodities that each one of these curves might represent.

4. Show on a diagram why elasticity is so important in determining price changes. (Refer back to the diagrams on p. 33 to be sure that you are right.)

5. Draw a diagram that shows what we mean by an increase in the quantity supplied; another diagram to show what is meant by an increase in supply. Now do the same for a decrease in quantity supplied and in supply. (Warning: it is very easy to get these wrong. Check yourself by seeing if the decreased supply curve shows the seller offering less goods at the same prices.) Now do the same exercise for demand.

6. How does substitution affect elasticity? If there are many substitutes for a product, is demand for it elastic or inelastic? Why?

7. Show on a diagram (or with figures) why you would rather be the seller of a good for which demand was elastic, if you were in a market with falling prices. Suppose prices were rising—would you still be glad about the elasticity of demand?

8. By and large, are luxuries apt to enjoy elastic or inelastic demands? Has this anything to do with their price? Can high-priced goods have inelastic demands?

9. Why is demand more apt to become elastic over time?

10. The price of pipe tobacco rises. What is apt to be the effect on the demand for pipes? On the demand for cigars?

11. What is meant by an orderly market? If prices fall, how should you behave as a buyer to insure an orderly market? As a seller? What might make you behave differently?

12. If we faced the prospect of a runaway inflation, what public statement would you advise the President to make?

4

The market
for factors

When we now look around at the hum of transactions on the marketplace, a great deal has become clear to us. We understand how prices are formed for the goods and services that are traded there, why and how those prices change, and the way in which changes are normally kept within bounds so that the system can maintain an orderly flow of output. We understand, as well, how those very same prices serve as rationing agencies for the society, distributing the output of the economy among those who are capable of paying for it.

But who *is* capable of paying for it? Through the market pass men and women in all walks of life, in all occupations, in all degrees of property ownership. Some are rich, some poor; some are very well treated by the market, some pushed aside by its operation. Does microeconomics shed light on this side of the market mechanism? Does it explain the causes of individual riches and poverty?

The distribution of income

Anyone who first looks at the realities of income distribution recognizes that there are some aspects of it that microeconomics has little to say about. At one end of the scale of income distribution are the 25 to 30 million individuals who as families have less than $60 a week; or as single individuals, less than $30; at the other end are the few hundred individuals whose incomes from property alone are over a million dollars each. Microeconomics does not enlighten us much concerning the root causes of these extremes of income. If we want to understand the reasons for poverty (particularly the poverty of the slums and of racially disprivileged groups), it is sociology and psychology and cultural anthropology to which we must turn rather than to price theory, while the presence of vast private fortunes requires us to learn about economic history and the workings of the law quite as much as about the operations of the market for factors.

Microeconomics, in other words, will not help us understand the origin or nature of incomes that have relatively little to do with the working of the market mechanism. Those who are outside the market framework in the enclaves of the slums, or those whose incomes represent the inheritance of great sums won in the past do not fall mainly within the microeconomic examination of the factor market. Yet, about the three-quarters or more of the population that lies above the poverty line and that enters the market regularly to earn its income, microtheory will tell us a good deal. If it cannot explain for any single individual exactly why his income is what it is, it will at least tell us what kinds of forces bear on his earning capacity, and therefore how changes in the market are likely to affect his economic future.

Land, labor, and capital

In a very general way we already know the answer to the problem of individual earnings. Men make what they make because they sell their services in the market for the factors of production and receive as their reward whatever price the market puts on their contribution.

This general explanation serves only to orient us to the more interesting and difficult aspects of the problem, but even the first view makes one important thing clear. It is that the market for factors is essentially one in which *productive services* are bought and sold. When a firm buys Labor, it does not (except in a slave economy) buy an actual human being. It hires him, which is a very different thing, for it means that it buys his labor only, and not the physical asset (his body) in which it is contained.

The same differentiation between productive services and assets must be noticed in the markets for Land and Capital. When a farmer buys land, what he is willing to pay for are the powers of fertility contained in the soil. True, in order to get the use of those powers, he may want to, or have to, buy the real estate itself. In that case, however, the price of the asset will depend entirely on the *yield* that the land is expected to produce. Suppose our farmer is hoping that land values themselves will rise. Then he is acting as a speculator rather than as a farmer and is betting that the value of the *future services* of that land (where perhaps he hopes one day a factory will stand) will be so much higher than the value of its present services, that values will increase. (If he is wrong in his guess, he will be saddled with very high-priced land for farming — a thought that explains a good deal of the ill-fortunes that have beset the American farmer from time to time.)

Does a manufacturer also buy the services of capital? Indeed he does. When he buys a machine, his demand for it will depend on his estimate of the present and future returns the machine will bring, so that the price he will offer derives directly from the value of the machine's services. Suppose he acquires money — that is, suppose he borrows funds from someone else? In that case the price he will pay for the temporary use of these funds — the *interest* cost — will certainly be governed by the present and prospective profits he expects to derive from using the money he has borrowed.*

Thus, when we speak of the market for factors we are actually talking about the value of their *services*. Clearly, there is a relation between the value of those services and the so-called capitalized value at which the asset itself sells for, but that is a complicated problem into which we need not go.

The supply curves of factors

What do we know about the willingness and ability of the owners of land, labor, and capital to offer their services on the marketplace at varying prices for these services?

Except for the important case of labor (about which more in a moment), we really do not know too much about the shapes of the individual supply curves of land and capital. Will a man with a certain capital sum be willing to lend more of it when interest goes up — or will he lend more when interest declines, so that he can get as much income as before? In the same way, will a typical landowner increase or decrease the amount he rents out as rentals rise and fall?

These questions are difficult to answer for the individual. For the community, however, they are simpler to deal with. A rising price of land tempts many owners of real estate who were not previously "in the market" to rent out their land or their rooms or their houses. So, too, a rising price of interest attracts savings from people who were formerly

---

*Is money itself a factor of production? Not in the technical sense of the term. Money can buy factors of production — land, labor, or capital goods — but it does not in itself contribute to output.

not interested in saving, or brings about switches of money from check-
ing accounts into interest-bearing accounts or securities.

The supply curve of labor

Hence we assume that aggregate supply curves of land and capital
have the normal upward rising and rightward sloping shapes. The individual *labor supply curve* is an interesting exception, however. As Fig.
4-1 shows us, it has a curious shape. Up to wave level *OA*, we have no
trouble explaining things. The curve simply tells us that normally we will
not be willing and able to work longer hours (i.e., to offer more of our
labor services within a given time period) unless we are paid more per
hour. Economists speak of the *increasing marginal disutility* of labor,
meaning by this that the bother and toil of work mounts after a time, so
that we will not labor long hours unless the reward per hour rises enough
to compensate us for our added pains.

How then do we explain the "backward-bending" portion of the rising
curve above wage level *OA*? The answer lies in adding to the rising
marginal disutility of labor the falling marginal utility of *income* itself, on
the assumption that an extra dollar of income to a man who is making
$10,000 is worth less than the utility of an additional dollar to a man
who is making $5,000.

Together, these two forces explain very clearly why the supply curve
of labor bends backward above a certain level. Take a man who has
been tempted to work 70 hours a week by wage raises that have finally
reached $5 an hour. Now suppose that wages go up another 10 per cent.
It is possible of course, that the marginal utility of the additional income
may outweigh the marginal disutility of these long hours, so that our man
stays on the job or even works longer hours. If, however, his marginal
utility of income has reached a low enough point and his marginal disutility of work a high enough point, the raise may bring a new possibility:
he may work *fewer* hours and enjoy the same (or a somewhat higher)
income as well as additional leisure. Thus, as his pay goes up 5 per cent,
he may reduce his workweek by 5 per cent.

Backward-bending supply curves help explain the long secular trend
toward reducing the workweek. Over the last century, weekly hours

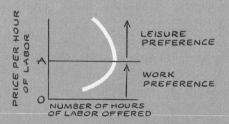

LEISURE
PREFERENCE

WORK
PREFERENCE

THE
BACKWARD-BENDING
SUPPLY CURVE
OF LABOR

PRICE PER HOUR
OF LABOR

A

O   NUMBER OF HOURS
OF LABOR OFFERED

FIG. 4-1

have decreased by about 40 per cent. Although many factors have con-verged to bring about this result, one of them has certainly been the desire of individual men and women to exchange the marginal utility of potential income for that of increased leisure.

Elasticities and mobility

These psychological considerations behind supply curves are the counterpart of the tastes and desires behind our demand curves. Yet, when we discussed demand, we found technical reasons, such as substi-tution and complementarity, as well as psychological ones, for the differing positions and shapes of demand curves. Are there technical reasons to be looked for also in explaining the nature of the supply curve of factors?

One such comes immediately to mind: the potential *geographic mobility* of factors. Suppose there is a sudden rise in the demand for labor in a particular locality. We would expect to witness a rise in the price of labor, at least for a while. But then the higher price of labor should serve to attract this factor of production from other areas, and in this way bring about a compensating increase in supply to mitigate or reverse the price rise.

Mobility is thus an enormously important technical condition affecting the shape and position of the labor supply curve. More than a million American families change addresses in a typical year, so that over a decade the normal mobility of the labor force can transport 15 to 20 million people (including wives and children) from one part of the coun-try to another. Without this potential influx of labor, we would expect wages to shoot up steeply whenever an industry in a particular locality expanded, with the result that further profitable expansion might then become impossible.

We also speak of mobility of labor in a vertical sense, referring to the movement from occupation to occupation. Here the barriers to mobility are not usually geographical but institutional (for instance, trade union restrictions on membership) or social (discrimination against the upward mobility of Negroes) or economic (the lack of sufficient income to gain a needed amount of education). Despite these obstacles, occupational mobility is also very impressive from generation to generation, as the astounding changes in the structure of the U.S. labor force have demon-strated.

Here again the upward streaming of the population in response to the inducement of better incomes makes the long-run elasticities of supply of favored professions much more elastic than they are in the short run. This is a force tending to reduce the differences between income ex-

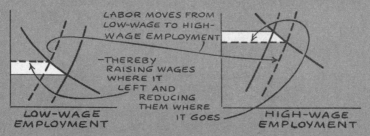

LABOR MOVES FROM LOW-WAGE TO HIGH-WAGE EMPLOYMENT

—THEREBY RAISING WAGES WHERE IT LEFT AND REDUCING THEM WHERE IT GOES

LOW-WAGE EMPLOYMENT

HIGH-WAGE EMPLOYMENT

FIG. 4-2

tremes, since the mobility of labor will not only shift the supply curve to the right in the favored places to which it moves (thereby exerting a downward pressure on incomes), but will move the supply curve to the left in those industries it leaves, bringing an upward impetus to incomes. Figure 4-2 shows how this process works.

Time and technical specificity

Mobility is by no means an attribute of labor alone. Take that seemingly least mobile of factors, land. In the very short run, the supply curve of land to any one industry is likely to be very inelastic. For example, if the orangegrowers of Florida want to increase their crop acreage within a year, they may find that it is very difficult to do so. But over a stretch of years, it is surprising how "mobile" the supply of land can become. Acres formerly devoted to other crops can be put into oranges. If the price of oranges goes high enough, it may even pay to reclaim land from urban or industrial use. To be sure, in the long run, the amount of land suitable for orangegrowing is limited, so that at some point the supply curve becomes totally inelastic. But over a very long intermediate range, land is in elastic supply. A graph of the short- and long-run supply curve of land for a given purpose would look like Fig. 4-3.

The example of land makes clear that it is not only geographic mobility but *technical specificity* that determines the responsiveness of a factor to changes in price. This helps explain why *time* plays such an important role in the elasticity of factor supply. Supply curves, like demand curves, are much more elastic over time because the process of redeploying factors from one use to another typically requires efforts that cannot be quickly brought to bear.

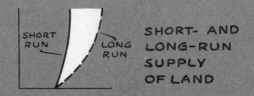

SHORT RUN

LONG RUN

SHORT- AND LONG-RUN SUPPLY OF LAND

FIG. 4-3

Suppose, for instance, that there is a sudden increase in the demand for steel products in the South and a simultaneous fall in the demand for lumber. In the short run there is not very much mobility that can be expected of the capital in these two industries. Lumber mills cannot be used to make steel. Hence the supply of steel mill services would be steeply inelastic. Over a period of time, however, the supply of capital, like land and labor, gains mobility. The lumber mills will eventually become depreciated or will be sold, and funds may thereupon be directed into steel. Or new mills will be built by funds supplied by other parts of the country. In other words, capital goods are usually limited in their flexibility of use, but money capital is tremendously mobile. In this way, the flow of money capital from one industry to another serves the same purpose as the flow of labor between employments, increasing the quantities of the factor where its price is rising, and diminishing it where it is not, in this way acting to keep the discrepancies between industries at a minimum.

Quasi rents

The importance of time in bringing about increases in factor supplies alerts us to a very important reason for the existence of very large incomes (and very large disparities of incomes) in the short run. This is the phenomenon of *quasi rent* (sometimes also called *economic rent*).

Quasi rents or economic rents are not the same as the rent on land, and the unfortunate fact that the terminology is so close has justifiably aggravated a good many generations of students. Hence let us begin by making a clear distinction between the two. *Rent is the payment we make to induce the owner of land to offer the services on the market.* If we cease to pay rent or pay less rent, the amount of land offered on the market will fall. If we pay more, it will rise. Thus rent is both a payment made to a factor of production to compensate its owner for its services, and an element of cost that must enter into the calculation of selling prices. If a farmer must pay $100 rent to get an additional field he needs, that $100 will clearly be part of the cost of producing his new crop.

Quasi rents or economic rents are different from this. *First, the term applies to all resources — land, labor, or capital goods. Second, it is not a return earned by the factor, in that the payment has nothing to do with inducing the factor to enter the market. Third, quasi rents are not a cost that helps to determine selling price, but they are earnings that are determined by selling price.* Let us see what these differences mean.

An illustration may help clarify the problem. Figure 4-4 shows the supply curve for first-class office space in New York City. Note that over a considerable range there is an unchanging price for space — evi-

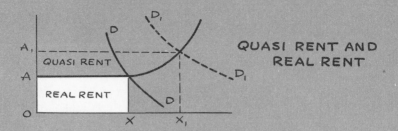

QUASI RENT AND
REAL RENT

FIG. 4-4

dently there is all the space anyone can want up to quantity OX at a price (determined, let us say, by given costs) OA. The receipts of land-lords—OA times OX—are real rent in the sense of being a necessary payment for the resources used. If no rent were paid, no space would be offered; as more is paid, more is forthcoming.

But now suppose that the demand for office space increases from DD to D_1D_1. The supply of space is now stretching thin, and additional first-class offices are hard to get, or expenditures are required to upgrade "second-class" space. The price rises accordingly from OA to OA_1.

Now we must differentiate carefully between rent and quasi rent. As the price rises, the quantity of space increases from OX to OX_1. Hence, for each unit of *additional* space the higher price was needed in order to bring that particular unit onto the market. But the higher price A_1 of space will not just apply to these new units. All "first-class office space" will go up in price. As a result, all the space represented by OX_1 will now receive a rental of OA_1, instead of OA. *But this increase in rental served no purpose in bringing these original units (OX) into the market. The additional revenue comes to them solely because the supply curve of which they are a part has become upward sloping. Thus economic rent or quasi rent is a return that accrues to factors by virtue of their scarcity, not by virtue of their contribution to output.*

Note also that the amount of quasi rent is determined by the selling price. At the margin of the supply curve, where supply and demand meet, the last unit of supply earns its full return (for it would not appear on the market for less), but all the previous intramarginal units are the benefi-ciaries of a situation in which they play no active role at all. If the supply curve becomes totally inelastic—if we simply run out of first-class office space—then quasi rents will be received by all units, including the marginal ones, as Fig. 4-5 makes clear.

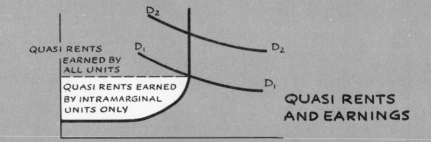

QUASI RENTS
AND EARNINGS

FIG. 4-5

Note carefully that the concept of quasi rent or economic rent is not limited to land. Take car rentals, for instance. Let us suppose that there is a going rate for cars, and that we can rent all the car transportation we need at that price. Suddenly there is a jump in demand, and the rentable car fleet is too small. Rentals will rise. If no additional cars come onto the market, the fleet owners will simply enjoy economic rents on all their cars. But quite possibly the rising rental will bring new cars into the supply curve: fleet owners will expand their fleets; or private owners may rent cars on their own. These marginal cars will be earning no more than the return required for their addition to the supply curve, so that we cannot call their earnings an economic rent. But the previous cars, all of which will enjoy the rise in rates, are the sources of quasi rents for their owners.

In the same way the earnings of actors or authors or of the owners of any scarce talent or skill are likely to be partly economic rents. An actress might be perfectly content to offer her services for a fine movie role for $50,000, but she may be able to get $100,000 for the part because of her "name." The first $50,000, without which she would not work, is her wage; the rest is an economic rent. So, too, a plumber who would be willing to work for standard wages, but who gets double because he is the only plumber in town, earns economic rents. And as we shall see in our next chapter, economic rent also helps to explain part of business profits.

The concept of economic rent gives us a much-needed insight into the cause of income differentials. Anything that inhibits the mobility of factors—anything that impedes their pursuit of self-interest by moving from lower to higher-paid occupations or localities—creates or perpetuates economic rents. Barriers of race and wealth, of patents and initiation fees, of geography and social custom—all give rise to shelters behind which economic rents flourish. Some of these barriers cannot be helped in the short run, and others may simply reflect the occasional virtuosity of a few performers: baseball stars and great painters both earn rents, not because they are the beneficiaries of factor immobility, but simply because they are unique performers whose output (supply curve) is fixed, and who therefore enjoy the rewards of a high demand. Many other rents, however, are the creations of artificial scarcity and can be remedied by removing these man-made barriers.

Economic rents are clearly a source of waste for society, for they reward factors more generously than is necessary for their services. Why do we not remove them, therefore, by price controls? The answer is that price controls would create a situation of "shortage" such as we discussed on p. 25. For instance, a price ceiling to prevent rented cars from earning quasi rents would force us to adopt some rationing system other than price, to determine who would get the available cars. Thus economic rents still serve a purpose in aiding the allocation tasks of the market.*

Supply curves and prices

Inelasticities of supply (and economic rents) help us to explain how some of the price adjustments we studied in the last chapter actually take place on the market.

Take the case of the increase in the demand for eggs. Suppose that housewives, for whatever reason, begin to buy larger quantities of eggs from their grocers. Most grocers will not raise prices, the way we have assumed that they will. Many small businesses price on a "mark-up" basis—adding a fixed percentage to the price charged them by their own suppliers. Hence when the demand for eggs rises, grocers will notice it only because their egg stocks run out, and their response will be only to order more eggs from their wholesale suppliers. Since wholesalers are prepared for such emergencies and have extra stock on hand, the higher demand of housewives can be accommodated without any increase in price, as Fig. 4-6 shows.

But now suppose that the higher demand of housewives persists for a week. Grocers keep renewing their larger egg orders, and wholesalers soon find themselves out of stock. They begin to place larger orders with the egg farmers who supply them. Here we encounter a situation with an *inelastic* supply. Presumably the egg farms are already shipping all their eggs, so that orders for additional quantities have no (or very little) effect on production, at least in the short run. Instead, egg prices on the farm will now go up, and egg farmers will earn economic rents on their chickens. We can see this in Fig. 4-7.

Note further that once egg prices have been raised by the farmer,

*Can we not remove economic rents by taxation? We can indeed, insofar as we are able to tax the original receiver of such a rent—for example, the movie actress or the original fleet owner. In the case of the car owner, however, his fleet may be sold to a second owner. In that case, the price of the cars when sold, will reflect their higher earnings, and the second owner, although presumably making normal profits, will no longer make a quasi rent. Hence economic rents are capturable by taxation only when the taxes affect the original beneficiary.

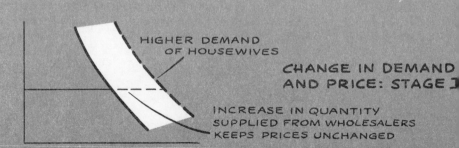

HIGHER DEMAND
OF HOUSEWIVES

CHANGE IN DEMAND
AND PRICE: STAGE I

INCREASE IN QUANTITY
SUPPLIED FROM WHOLESALERS
KEEPS PRICES UNCHANGED

FIG. 4-6

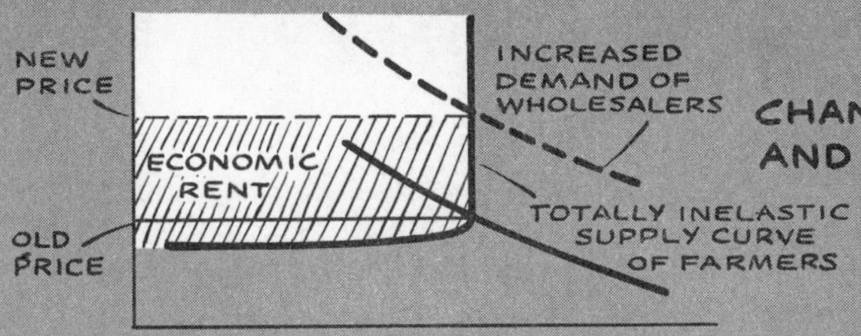

NEW PRICE

ECONOMIC RENT

OLD PRICE

INCREASED DEMAND OF WHOLESALERS

TOTALLY INELASTIC SUPPLY CURVE OF FARMERS

CHANGE IN DEMAND AND PRICE: STAGE II

FIG. 4-7

costs go up to wholesalers, who must now raise the price of eggs to grocers, who in turn will pass along the boost to consumers. If the housewife then asks the grocer why egg prices are higher, the grocer will answer perfectly correctly that "costs are up." And so they are— because demand is up. The cause of the whole change in prices has been the increased demand of the housewife, but the mechanism for raising prices has involved a series of markets, with the kingpin market that in which supplies were inelastic.*

The demand for the factors of production

We have come to understand something of the complex forces at work in the factor market, where the incomes that will buy the wares in the goods market are generated. But our explanation is obviously incomplete until we have looked into the demand for factors as well as their supply.

In part, we already understand the demand for factors from our previous chapters. A portion of the labor force, or of land, or capital is demanded directly by consumers for their own personal enjoyment, exactly the same as a good or service. This kind of demand for factors of production takes the guise of the demand for lawyers and barbers and servants, or the demand for plots of land for personal dwellings, or as the demand for cars and washing machines and the like that consumers hold as personal capital goods. To the extent that factors are demanded directly for such consumer purposes, there is nothing that differs in analyzing the price they receive from the price of any good.

Take the price of dental services, for example, which obviously determines much of the income of dentists. We can draw a demand curve for dentists' services which will certainly slope downward (and will probably be highly income- and price-elastic), and we can draw a supply curve of dentists' services which, in the short run anyway, will probably be fairly inelastic and perhaps backward sloping. Figure 4-8 then shows us how much a typical dentist makes.

*I have adapted this example from Armen A. Alchian and William R. Allen, *University Economics* (Belmont, Calif.: Wadsworth Publishing Co., Inc., 1964), p. 105f., one of the best expositions of the market mechanism I have ever seen.

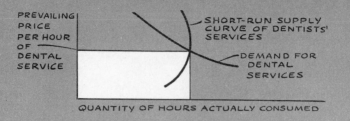

FIG. 4-8

PREVAILING PRICE PER HOUR OF DENTAL SERVICE

SHORT-RUN SUPPLY CURVE OF DENTISTS' SERVICES

DEMAND FOR DENTAL SERVICES

QUANTITY OF HOURS ACTUALLY CONSUMED

DEMAND AND SUPPLY FOR LABOR CONSUMED AS A SERVICE

Comparative earnings

Now suppose that we compare the prices per hour of a number of occupations in which demand stems directly from the consumer, and we find the result to look like Table 4-1.

TABLE 4 • 1

	Price per hour
Lawyers	$10
Dentists	8
Barbers	4
Baby-sitters	1

How can we explain the differentials we find? Part of the answer lies in the differently shaped and located demand curves for these different services. What we must know, in other words, is the amount of money a consumer of a given income level is willing to spend for different quantities of the services of lawyers, dentists, barbers, and baby-sitters, and also the elasticities of his demand curves for these various services.

But a knowledge of the pattern of demand only sets the stage. We also need to know why the supply curve of different occupations is differently located and why each has the shape it does. And here we must look in particular for reasons that make some supply curves more inelastic than others over the long run—that is, reasons that prevent labor from moving out of low-paid occupations such as baby-sitting or barbering into high paid ones like dentistry and the legal profession.

We are already alerted to the role that institutional and social barriers to mobility can play here, so that we recognize some of the income differential we see as an *economic rent*. But that is not the whole story. Part of the difference in the pay of two occupations may also reflect *different estimates of its marginal disutility*. Thus dangerous work typically pays a premium over safe work, because the higher disutility of dangerous work requires an additional incentive to attract labor to it. It is interesting to reflect that in a world without any barriers to occupational mobility at all, dangerous and dirty work would command the highest remuneration in the society, and easy and pleasant work the lowest. In such a world coal miners would make much more than law-

yers, for there would be a flood of labor into law and a general exodus of labor from coal mining, with the expected effects on the market price of each. That is why one effect of prosperity is to raise the relative wages of "dirty work," since good times tend to improve mobility and thereby enable workers in low-grade occupations to move laterally or vertically to better ones.

But there is still another ingredient in determining the differential of incomes. This is the *investment that different occupations require.* It takes very little training to be a baby-sitter; a fair amount to be a barber; a lot to be a dentist or lawyer. The investment expenditures for these different occupations take the form, mainly, of education—which is one reason why it seems odd to classify education as a consumers' good in the national income accounts. Nevertheless, the point is that the money that has been poured into a long education must be expected to earn a return: therefore, part of the higher incomes of trained people consists really of interest on the capital sums invested in their careers. Here, of course, is where the underlying distribution of wealth affects the distribution of income, for the sons of the rich have better chances than those of the poor in investing in their own futures.

Finally there is the plain fact of *the differences in human abilities.* Here there is an interesting bit of corroborative evidence. We believe that the distribution of abilities for nearly all skills follows the well-known "bell curve," with a few people at the very low and the very talented ends of the scale and with most people grouped evenly around a middle point, as Fig. 4-9 shows.

Yet when we study the distribution of incomes within a given trade (such as weekly industrial earnings), we usually find that the distribution is "skewed," with most of the individuals clustered at the low end of the scale (Fig. 4-10).

This would seem to deny the validity of the effect of ability on earnings—until we make an adjustment in the scale on which we plot earnings. Instead of measuring them on a regular arithmetic scale, we must plot them on a *proportional* (logarithmic) scale which gives equal emphasis to equal percentages of changes, as shown in Fig. 4-11.

NUMBER OF PEOPLE

"SKEWED" CURVE OF
WAGE DISTRIBUTION

LOW PAY   HIGH PAY

FIG. 4-10

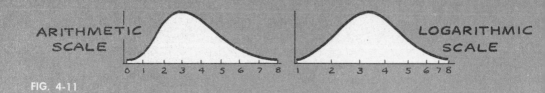

ARITHMETIC SCALE

LOGARITHMIC SCALE

FIG. 4-11

Then we discover that the distribution of earnings does indeed show a bell configuration that reflects the distribution of underlying abilities.*

Causes of income disparity

What conclusion can we then reach about the reasons for disparities of incomes, at least in those occupations in which demand stems directly from the consumer? We have seen that these disparities stem from two sets of causes, one transient and one not.

The transient—but very powerful—reasons involve all those social barriers that hinder the movement of factors from low-paid to high-paid employments and uses. Wealth on the one hand, prejudice and discrimination on the other are probably the main roots of differences in the capacity to move vertically or geographically or occupationally. Insofar as these impediments are social, however, they are capable of being by-passed or leveled, and indeed, the history of Western society is marked by a slow but gradual demolition of traditional or hereditary barriers and of a gradual opening of achievement to all talents.

There are, however, still more deep-seated reasons for variations in earnings in the differing marginal disutilities in which the spectrum of occupations is held, and in the differing "innate" abilities of men. We must conclude that in a world where the social barriers of privilege had been finally dismantled, differences would still be observed in the levels of reward, although they would probably be very unlike those we see today.

Property income

Note that these explanations involve only labor (in all its range of skills) and do not compare incomes earned by labor and those earned by capital or land. Microtheory can tell us why capital in one industry is more profitable than in another (there may be difficulties in mobility, for instance, that impede the flow of capital into the high-earnings industry), or why land brings different prices in different localities or times. But it cannot compare the income of a landowner or that of a capitalist with an

*See E. H. Phelps Brown, *The Economics of Labor* (New Haven: Yale University Press, 1962), pp. 154, 156.

income earned purely from work. This is because the ownership of assets in a market system is not realistically to be pictured as the result of a race for wealth that each generation conducts anew from an impartial starting line, but reflects to a large degree inequalities of private property formed in the past and perpetuated by inheritance. Here we are forced to return to the perspective of economic history to evaluate the sources of this wealth and its probable distribution in the future.

One reflection in this regard is interesting and germane. When we trace the over-all division of the social product between the share going to property and that going to labor (of all skills), we find the property share to have fallen slightly since the beginning of the twentieth century. In the decade 1900–1909, corporate profits and all interest and rent took 21.4 per cent of national income; in the 1960's, this has slipped to under 19 per cent. These measures are far from exact, but they suggest that the rewards to property are certainly not growing.

Entrepreneurial demand

There remains only the last, but most important aspect of factor pricing—the case in which demand arises not from a consumer but from a firm. What is the difference? It is that when a consumer hires a factor, he does so because of the personal enjoyments—the utilities—he will gain from doing so. No such consideration affects the entrepreneur's decision to buy factor services. When a businessman enters the factor markets, he does so not because land, labor, or capital will afford him increased utilities, but because using those factors will bring profits to his firm. Thus, unlike the direct demand of a consumer, the firm's demand for factors is a *derived demand*.

How much will a business man pay for a factor's services? We can see that the answer must have something to do with how much the factor is worth to him and that, in turn, this will involve the productivity of the factor—its contribution to output. But these questions bring us to the last of the processes by which the market system is knit together. We are finally ready to invade the precincts of the firm.

Summary

1. The rewards to land, labor, and capital are paid for the *services* that each offers on the market.
2. The supply curves of individual landowners and capitalists are indeterminate. But the supply curve for land or for capital in the aggregate is probably upward sloping, since a rise in price attracts new land and capital into the market.

3. The labor supply curve is typically *backward bending* above a certain price. This reflects the *increasing marginal disutility of work* and the *diminishing marginal utility of income.*

4. The elasticity of factor supply curves depends in large part on the *mobility of factors.* This is affected by geographical considerations, although more importantly by social and technical barriers and by the unequal distribution of wealth.

5. *Quasi rents* are an important constituent of earnings in all cases in which mobility is impaired. Quasi rents must be differentiated from *rents* in that they have nothing to do with increasing the supply of a factor on the market. Quasi rents can be found in many labor, land, and capital earnings. *Quasi rents are determined by price,* rather than helping to determine the price, as is the case with true rent.

6. Insofar as the demand for factors issues directly from consumers, we can explain factor earnings (incomes) by simple supply and demand analysis. In this case, however, we must note the following causes for differentials in incomes:

   • *Different marginal disutilities* of different employments
   • The different *amounts of investment* required for different occupations
   • Underlying differences in *abilities*

7. *Property incomes* cannot be compared directly with factor incomes. There is some evidence that property incomes are slowly declining as a claimant on national income.

8. Entrepreneurial demand for labor, unlike that of consumers, is *derived demand.* It depends on the expected profitability of hiring labor, not on the utilities to be enjoyed from it.

Questions

1. When a suburban homeowner buys "land," what services is he actually buying? When he hires domestic help, what services is he buying? When he borrows money from a bank?

2. Suppose you had $10,000 and that you had invested half of it at 6 per cent. If the rate of interest went up to 7 per cent would you be tempted to invest more? Or the same? Or might you think that it would be wise to invest a little less, since your income was now higher? Are there reasonable arguments for all three?

3. What do you think the supply curve of executive labor looks like? Is it backward bending? Would you expect it to be more or less backward bending than the supply curve of common labor? Why?

4. What do you think are the main impediments to factor mobility in the labor market? Location? Education? Discrimination? Wealth? How would you lessen these barriers?

5. How technically "specific" is a printing press? A lathe? In the long run, how can the capital in a printing press be moved from one use to another?

6. Exactly what is meant by rent? Does rent have something to do with the quantity of land offered on the market? What is quasi rent? If quasi rents go up, does this mean that more of a good is being offered?

7. What is meant by saying that rent is price-determining and that quasi rent is price-determined? Show the answer in a diagram.

8. Trace the consequences of a rise in the demand for beef on the price of beef. What have the various elasticities of supply of different stages in beef production to do with the eventual effect of a rise in demand on price?

9. Draw a supply and demand diagram for domestic help. What changes in demand or supply might affect domestics' wages? To what extent would you explain the relatively low level of domestics' wages in terms of marginal disutility? Lack of wealth? Investment?

10. In a world without any disparities in inherited wealth, what trends would you expect to find in the occupational differences in income? Would any income differences remain among occupations? Within occupations? What would each be traceable to?

5

The firm in the factor market

Even the most superficial acquaintance with the American economy tells us there are enormous discrepancies in size among business units. On the one hand, some ten million proprietorships in the U.S., many of them tiny, provide much of the service activities we use. On the other, a small group of gigantic private organizations, some of them rarely encountered in daily economic life, provide most of the industrial equipment we use. Between these extremes in the economic scale there is striking disparity of economic weight. U.S. Steel alone has assets equal to some 250,000 of these small business units; General Motors is worth half a million of them; A.T.&T., a million.

No realistic appraisal of the American economy can overlook this tremendous inequality of economic power. Yet the predominance of big business, most important for anyone who wishes to understand the economic history (past or future) of our country, does not help us much if we have a different aim in mind—to discover how our market system works. Surprisingly, the market mechanism illumines the operations of giant firms as much as the actions of small firms. Hence for the moment we are going to ignore the salient reality of big business and concern ourselves with the other end of the business scale. We are going to learn how the market mechanism works in a world of small competitive enterprises. In due course we will return to the "real" world and inquire what difference the fact of large size makes to the outcome of our theoretical study.

In addition to limiting our scrutiny to markets made up of small, competitive firms, we will add two assumptions about the behavior of these firms—one of them realistic and one perhaps not. The unrealistic assumption is that our firm acts *intelligently and rationally* in the pursuit of its goals. Since the world is littered with the bankruptcies that result from mistaken calculations and foolish decisions, this assumption may strain our credulity, but at least it will do no violence to understanding the *principles* of the market system.

Second, we will assume that our firm is motivated by a desire to *maximize its profits in the short run*—that is, day by day. Later, when we study the operations of very large firms we shall have to ask whether this maximizing assumption makes much sense in their case. But when we deal with the "atomistic" competition of small firms, the assumption stands up very well *because as we shall see, it is only by trying to maximize short-term profits that small firms manage to survive at all.* This gives to microtheory the same two-sided relevance that we noted in the case of its description of the competitive market. Microtheory tells us how small firms actually do behave—and thereby enables us to make predictions about the way the market system works—and it also serves as a goal-oriented description of how small business firms *should* conduct their affairs if they hope to survive.

The problem of scale

What are the problems and pressures that beset the small firm in its fight for survival? They will become gradually clear to us as we move along. But at the outset one problem attracts our attention not only because it is unresolved from our last chapter, but because it bears directly on the ability of the firm to make profits. This is how a firm decides how many factors to hire and in what proportions to combine them.

Suppose, for example, that we are considering opening a bookstore. The first question that we will have to answer is how much land, labor, and capital we will need in the form of space that we rent, help that we hire (including ourselves), and equipment or inventories of books that we must have. No matter what business we are in, there will be some minimum size below which we know we cannot operate profitably. A bookstore may be very small, but it has to have *some* reasonable number of books on the premises, and it must have at least one person around to sell them. If we were in a somewhat more technical line of work—say, manufacturing plastic parts—we would base the minimum size of our plant on the machinery that would be essential for our operation. If we were in a highly complex mass assembly business, such as typewriters, the *smallest* efficient plant might run into an investment of millions of dollars and would require a work force of thousands of people. But that would take us well out of the world of atomistic competition to which we are still devoting our attention.

In other words, the first decision about the hiring of factors involves the choice of *scale,* and that choice, it can be seen, is basically determined by the prevailing technology. In every kind of business there is usually a minimum size of establishment below which it is impossible to operate competitively because one of the factors would not be present in large enough quantity to allow certain technical efficiencies to be realized. This fact, in turn, arises because factors are not infinitely divisible for all uses—there is always a minimum amount of one factor that must be applied if a certain output is to be secured. In agriculture, for example, this minimum may be established by requirements of acreage; in manufacturing it is likely to be set by the irreducible requirements of the needed capital equipment. It is simply not possible to build an automobile plant that will fit into a cigar store or to raise cattle in a suburban back yard.

The factor mix

But once the minimum size of our enterprise has been established, we know the amount of only *one* factor we will have to hire if we are to open shop. Suppose that the limiting factor is land and that we decide that the smallest profitable bookstore would have to have at least 500 square feet of space. There is still the question of how much of the other factors we are to add to the predetermined factor of land. Assuming that we had $10,000 to spend, where should we put our money—into a large inventory of books and a small sales and office force (perhaps only ourselves), or into two or more salespeople working with a smaller inventory of books?

This question involves us not in a determination of the scale of the enterprise, but of the *mix of factors* that will be most profitable within a given scale. To go back to our plastics manufacturer for a moment, assume that he decides what the minimum investment in machinery will be for a profitable operation. He will then have to decide whether to spend relatively more money on land or on labor. Perhaps he has a choice of building his plant in two areas—one in which land is expensive but labor abundant, another where land is very cheap but labor is dearer. Which should he choose?

The answer to these problems takes us back to consider an attribute of the factors of production that we have been able to overlook until now, because we were considering their output as if it were a consumers' good to be directly enjoyed. *When a factor is being hired by a firm, the firm considers the usefulness of that factor as a means to an end—* the end being the output of its own product, be that the sale of books or plastics. Therefore it is the *profitability of the factor* that interests the businessman who is considering which factor to hire. If land will produce more business for him than labor, he will hire land. If a sales clerk will sell more books for us than having a larger inventory of books, we will hire a sales clerk. The question is, how do we know which factor will be the better buy?

The productivity curve: increasing returns

As we shall see, this is by no means a simple question to answer, for many considerations bear on the decision to hire a factor or not, or on the choice of one factor over another. But in the center of any business-man's calculations lies one extremely important fact to which we must now pay close attention. This is the physical productivity of different factors—their capacity to increase his output—and more than that, *the changing physical productivity that results from combining different amounts of one factor with fixed amount of the others.*

Let us begin with a case that is very simple to imagine. Suppose we have a farmer who has a farm of 100 acres and a certain amount of equipment, and no labor at all. Now let us picture our farmer first hiring one man, then a second man of the same abilities, then a third, and so on. Obviously, the output of the farm would grow. What we want to find out, however, is whether it will grow in some clearly defined pattern that we can trace to the changing amounts of the factor that is being added.

What would such a curve of productivity look like? Assume that one man, working the 100 acres alone as best he can, produces 1,000 bush-els of grain. A second man, helping the first, should be enormously valuable, because two men can begin to specialize and divide the work, each doing the jobs he is better at and saving the time formerly wasted by moving from one job to the next. As a consequence, output may jump to 3,000 bushels. Since the *difference* in output is 2,000 bushels, we speak of the *marginal productivity* of labor, when two men are working, as 2,000 bushels. Note that we should not (although in carelessness we sometimes do) speak of the marginal productivity of the second *man*. Alone, his efforts are no more productive than those of the first man: if we fired the first man, worker number 2 would only produce 1,000 bushels. What makes the difference is the jump in the combined produc-tivity of the *two* men, once specialization can be introduced. Hence we should speak of the changing marginal productivity of *labor*, not of the individual.

It is not difficult to imagine an increasing specialization taking place with the third, fourth, and fifth man, so that the addition of another unit of labor input in each case brings about an output larger than was real-ized by the average of all the previous men. Remember that this does not mean the individual factor units themselves are more productive. *It means that as we add units of one factor, the total mix of these units* *plus the fixed amounts of other factors, forms an increasingly efficient technical combination.**

We call the range of factor inputs, over which average productivity rises, a range of *increasing average returns.* It is, of course, a stage of production that is highly favorable for the producer. Every time he adds a factor, efficiency rises. (As a result, as we shall see in our next chapter, costs per unit of output fall.) The rate of increase will not be the same, for the initial large marginal leaps in productivity will give way to smaller ones—that is, marginal output is actually falling. But the over-all trend of productivity, whether we measure it by looking at *total* output or at *average* output per man, will still be up. And all this keeps on happening, of course, because the factor we are adding has not yet reached its point of maximum technical efficiency with the given amount of the other factors.

Diminishing returns

Then our farmer notices a disconcerting phenomenon. At a certain point, average productivity no longer rises when he adds another man. Total output will still be rising with the addition of more men, but a quick calculation reveals that the last man on the team has added so little to the productivity of the farm that *average* output per man has actually fallen.

What has happened has been that we have overshot the point of maximum technical efficiency, and that labor is now beginning to "crowd" the land or the equipment. Opportunities for further specialization have become nonexistent—worse yet, additional labor is forced to perform so inefficiently that the *average* output of the whole labor force is pulled down. We *call this state of falling average performance a condition of decreasing average returns.* As the words suggest, we are getting back less and less as we add the critical factor—not only from the "marginal" man, but from the average efforts of all the men. (Now, of course, costs will be rising per unit.) If we went on foolishly adding men, eventually the addition of another worker would add nothing to total output. In fact, the next worker might then so disrupt the factor mix that *total* output would actually fall and we would be in a condition of negative returns.

*With each additional man, the proportions of land, labor, and capital are altered, so that the change in the level of output should rightfully be ascribed to new levels of efficiency resulting from the interaction of *all three factors.* But since labor is the factor whose input we are varying, it has become customary to call the change in output the result of a change in "labor productivity." If we were altering land or capital alone, we would call the change the result of changes in their productivities, even though, as with labor the real cause is the changing efficiency of *all* factors in different mixes.

TABLE
5 • 1

Number of men	Total output	Marginal productivity* (change in output)	Average productivity (total output ÷ no. of men)
1	1,000	1,000	1,000
2	3,000	2,000	1,500
3	5,500	2,500	1,833
4	7,800	2,300	1,950
5	9,800	2,000	1,960
6	11,600	1,800	1,930
7	13,100	1,500	1,871
8	14,300	1,200	1,790

*Note that *marginal* productivity begins to diminish with the third man (who adds only 500, not 1,000, bushels to output). *Average* productivity rises until the fifth man, however. This is because marginal productivity for men numbers 3, 4, and 5, although diminishing steadily, is still high enough to raise average output.

This changing profile of physical productivity is one of the most important generalizations about the real world that economics makes. It will help us to think it through if we now study the relationships of marginal and average productivity and of total output in a schedule (Table 5-1) and a graph (Fig. 5-1):

The three curves in Fig. 5-1 actually all show the same thing, only in different ways. The top curve shows us that as we add men to our farm, output at first rises very rapidly, then slowly, then actually declines. The marginal productivity curve shows us *why* this is happening to total output: as we add men, the contribution they can make to output changes markedly, at first each man adding enough so that average output grows, finally each man adding so little that he actually pulls down the average that obtained before his hiring. And the average curve, as we have just indicated, merely sums up the over-all output in an arithmetical way by showing us what the average person contributes to it.

Put into the form of a generalization, we can say that *as we add successive units of one factor to fixed amounts of others, the average output of the units of the variable factor will at first rise and then decline. We call this the law of variable proportions or the law of diminishing returns, or we can simply talk about it as the physical productivity curve.*

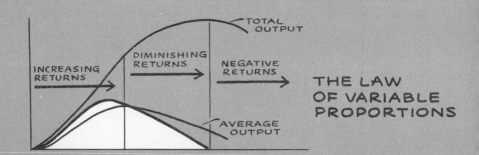

FIG. 5-1

The law of variable proportions

The generalizations of the law of variable proportions constitute one of the key insights that a study of microeconomics gives us into the workings of the real world. Hence let us be certain that we understand exactly what the law says and implies.

1. The law of variable proportions describes what happens to physical productivity when we add units of one factor and *hold the others constant*. As we added labor in the example above, we did not also add land or capital. Had we done so, there would have been no way of ascribing changes in output to the addition of one factor rather than the other.

2. The law applies to the additions of *any* factor to fixed quantities of the others. Suppose that we had started with a fixed amount of labor and capital and had added successive acres of land. The first acre would not have been very productive, for we would have had to squeeze too much labor and capital into its area. The second acre would have permitted a better utilization of all three factors, and so "its" marginal productivity would have been much higher. But in time the addition of successive units of land would pass the point of optimum mix, until another acre would add so little yield that the average production of all acres would be pulled down. And the same pattern of increase, diminution, and final decrease would of course attend the addition of doses of capital — say successive bags of fertilizer or additional tractors — to a fixed amount of land and labor.

3. Unlike many other "laws" in economics, the law of variable proportions has nothing to do with behavior. The actions of men on the marketplace, or the impulses or restraints of utility and disutility, play no role in diminishing returns. *Essentially, the law expresses a constraint imposed by the laws of nature.* If there were no such constraint, we could grow all the food required by the world in a single acre, or even a flowerpot, simply by adding more and more labor and capital.

Economics, as we have occasion to remark a number of times, is the study of how men seek to provision themselves, of how society solves the universal problem of production and distribution. Through most of this book we have been concerned with the *social* aspects of this problem — with the difficulties in arranging the institutional and behavioral requirements for survival and growth. It is well to bear in mind that nature also imposes its conditions on man, and nowhere more visibly than in the diminishing returns that ultimately hamper all his efforts.*

*This technological or physical reason behind the law of diminishing returns is essentially the same as the one behind the law of increasing costs. In the case of the first law, we are interested in learning why the marginal output of a given good decreases as a single factor is added to given quantities of other factors; in the second, we want to know why the marginal output of a given good decreases when we shift *all factors* from other uses to produce that good. In both cases the critical element lies in the fact that technology or nature decrees a certain "mix" as the optimal resource combination for making any good. When we move factors from one use to another, sooner or later we encounter one factor that will become scarce relative to the others. From that point on, additional units of resources cannot be employed at maximal efficiency, and marginal output must fall.

Marginal revenue and marginal cost

But now we must get back to our point of interest—the firm seeking to hire factors to its own best advantage. Is a knowledge of factor productivity all a businessman needs? To revert to our first illustration, suppose we knew that a single salesclerk in our bookstore had a productivity of (i.e., could sell) 5 books a day. Would that alone tell us if we should hire him?

The question answers itself. Before we can hire the clerk or any other factor, we have to know two other things: (1) *we have to know what the unit of the factor will cost,* and (2) *we have to know how much revenue our firm will get as a result of hiring that unit of the factor.*

For instance, if the price of a salesclerk is $6,000 and if we think his activity as a salesperson will add 5 books a day to our sales, at an average price per book of $5, then if he works for 250 days, he will bring in revenues of $6,250 (5 × $5 × 250). Obviously it will pay to hire him.* On the other hand, if his productivity were less—if he sold only 4 books per day—then the revenues from hiring him would be only $5,000 (4 × $5 × 250), or $1,000 less than his wage. He would be a dead loss.

Our illustration enables us to see the general process by which entrepreneurs make their hiring decisions, and also enables us to see how productivity fits into those decisions. Whenever we are considering hiring any factor, we compare in our minds two sums. On the one hand, any increase in the units of the factor we hire will raise our cost. On the other hand, that same increased use of one factor should increase our output, and therefore our revenue. The conclusion is very simple. *If the marginal revenue expected from the addition of a unit of a factor is greater than the marginal cost of a unit of the factor, it pays to hire it. If the marginal cost is greater than the marginal revenue, it does not.* (Furthermore, it may even raise our profits if we fire factors, provided that in each case we reduce our costs by more than we reduce our revenues.)

Productivity and profit

Just where does productivity fit into this picture? The answer is that productivity tells us how much additional physical output we can get from hiring additional units of a factor. Thus, if we know what the unit of the factor will cost and what the sales price of our output will be, it is productivity that determines whether a factor will be worth its hire or not.

---

*For simplicity's sake, we assume that the bookstore gets its books free. We will take up the problem of business costs in our next chapter.

Let us see how this actually works in practice. In the schedules below we go back to our farm, this time armed with two new pieces of information. We know that labor costs $4,500 per man and that a bushel of wheat sells for $2.50. (Later we will look into *how* we know these things, but now we can take them for granted.) Our farm schedule of marginal cost and marginal revenue therefore looks like Table 5-2.

**TABLE
5 • 2**

Number of men	Marginal cost per man @ $4,500.	Marginal output per man (from Table 5-1)	Marginal revenue per man (output × $2.50)	Marginal profit or loss per man
1	$4,500	1,000	$2,500	−3,000
2	4,500	2,000	5,000	500
3	4,500	2,500	6,250	1,750
4	4,500	2,300	5,750	1,250
5	4,500	2,000	5,000	500
6	4,500	1,800	4,500	0
7	4,500	1,500	3,750	− 750
8	4,500	1,200	3,000	−1,500

What does our table tell us? Our first man seems to be very unprofitable, for he costs us $4,500 and brings in only $2,500. We suspect, however, that he is so inefficient because he is trying to spread his one unit of labor over the whole farm. The addition of a second man confirms our suspicions. He also costs us $4,500, but brings in $5,000. (Remember it is not the second man himself who does so, but the two men working together who give rise to an increase in revenues of that amount.) The third and fourth and fifth men also show profits, but when we reach the sixth man, the law of diminishing returns brings its decisive force to bear. The sixth man is unable to increase the productivity of the team by more than $4,500, which is just his hire. It is not worthwhile to engage him.

Are we certain that hiring five men will really maximize the profits of the farm? We can find out by adding up our *total* costs and our *total* revenues and figuring our profit at each level of operation.* (We get the totals by adding each marginal increment to the preceding sum of costs or revenues.)

---

*We are really fooling ourselves when we "check" on our former calculations about marginal changes by looking at the totals. For the totals are themselves nothing but the sum of the marginal changes! As long as each man brings *some* addition to revenue, large or small (that is, so long as marginal revenue is larger than marginal cost when that man is hired), then the total of all revenues must be growing larger too. When we add up the marginal contributions, we measure each different-sized contribution. We should not consider it a triumph when we discover that the whole contains the sum of what we put into it.

**TABLE
5 • 3**

Number of men	Total cost of men¹	Total revenue	Profit (total revenue less cost)
1	$ 4,500	$ 2,500	−$2,000
2	9,000	7,500	− 1,500
3	13,500	13,750	250
4	18,000	19,500	1,500
5	22,500	24,500	2,000
6	27,000	29,000	2,000
7	31,500	32,750	1,250
8	35,000	35,750	750

As we can see, our best profit comes with the hire of 5 men. The addition of a sixth does us no good. A seventh lowers our net income — not for any lack of skill or effort on his part, but because with seven men the mix of labor and the fixed amounts of other factors is no longer so efficient as before.

We can also see now how neatly the physical productivity curve ties together marginal cost and marginal revenue. For three things would entice us to hire the sixth or even the seventh man.

1. *A fall in cost.* If wages drop to any figure under $4,500, our sixth man will immediately pay his way. By how much would they have to drop to make it worthwhile to hire the seventh man? Marginal revenue when seven men are working is only $3,750. The wage level would have to drop below that point to bring a profit from seven men.

2. *A rise in the price of output.* If the demand for grain increased, and the price of grain went to $3, our calculations would change again. Now the sixth man is certainly profitable: adding him now brings a marginal revenue of 1,800 bushels × $3 or $5,400, far above his wage. Is the seventh man profitable? His physical productivity is 1,500 bushels. At $3 per bushel he is not quite worth hiring. At $3.01 he would be.

3. *An increase in productivity.* If a change in skills or techniques raises the physical output of each man, this will also change the margin of profitable factor use. Any small increase will lead to the employment of the sixth man.*

The choice among factors

We have talked, so far, as if an entrepreneur had only one "scarce" factor, and as if his only task were to decide how much of that factor to

---

*We can see that an increase in productivity leads to an increase in employment in the case of an individual firm. But we cannot generalize that an increase in the productivity of *all* workers will lead to an increase in total employment. That depends on what happens to aggregate demand or to the structure of employment.

add. But that is not quite the problem faced by the businessman. He has to make up his mind not only *whether* to add to his output at all, but *which* factor to hire in order to do so.

How does a businessman make such a choice? How would we choose between adding a salesclerk to our bookstore or adding inventory, or how would our farmer decide between hiring labor or spending the same sum on capital or land? Suppose that our farmer has already hired four men to work for him and has also rented a certain amount of land and used a certain amount of capital. Now when he thinks about expanding output he needs to know not only how much the addition of another man will yield him, but *what the alternatives are.*

They might look like this:

1. He can hire a fifth worker for $4,500 who will, as we know, bring about an increase in revenues of $5,000.
2. He could hire an acre of land for $500 which would increase his output by, say, 240 bushels, worth (@2.50) $600.
3. He could hire a tractor for $2,000 that would increase his output by 1,000 bushels worth $2,500.

Which, if any, should he choose? The first thing our farmer will have to do is to put these alternatives on a common footing so that he can compare the revenues he will get for a dollar's worth of each factor. He figures it this way:

1. For $4,500 spent on labor, he gets back $5,000, or a return of $1.11 for each $1 spent.
2. For $500 spent on land, he gets back $600, or a return of $1.20 per dollar.
3. For $2,000 spent on capital, he gets back $2,500 or a return of $1.25 per dollar outlay.

It is clear what our farmer should do. He should spend his money on tractors, not on land or labor — at least so long as the relative prices and productivities of the three factors remain unchanged.

Bidding for factors

But will factor prices remain unchanged? The question brings us back to the answered query of our last chapter: how are factor prices determined when firms, rather than consumers, provide the demand? We have taken a long detour into productivity because we could see that productivity was inextricably entangled in the firm's calculations as it bid for factors. But it was just this, the outcome of this bidding process, that we wanted to track down in the first place. Now we should be in a position to do so. We must begin by examining a critical supposition about factor pricing that we have already introduced very quietly. You will remember we assumed that our farmer was able to bid for additional land, or for any other factor, *without thereby affecting its price*.

Why were we able to make this assumption? The answer follows from the premise of atomistic firms from which we started. The amount of land or labor or capital that such a small firm can add to its operations is so insignificant a portion of the total supply of that factor that the individual firm's demand does not affect the price of the factor at all. If there are 100,000 young women looking for work as salesclerks in New York City, the addition of a few salesclerks in any single business will not change the "going" price for clerks at all. Nor will the demand of a small farmer, by itself, alter the rent of land, nor the demand for capital by a firm change the rate of interest.

In other words, the supply curve of any factor to one small firm looks like a horizontal line. It is infinitely elastic, because a firm can engage all of the factor it requires at the going price without thereby affecting the price of that factor at all.

But this is not the case when many small firms all begin to demand the same factor. If all stores are looking for salesclerks, the wage for clerks will rise. If many farmers seek land or capital, rentals or interest rates (or the prices of capital goods) will go up. As a result, each individual firm will find that the "going price" for the factor in general demand has a mysterious tendency to rise, as Fig. 5-2 shows.*

In other words, supply and demand sets the prices of factors, just as it does when consumers buy them, but now the demand is that exercised by a whole cluster of firms or by an industry. The individual firm has no impact on the market and no choice but to accept its price as given.

Factor pricing

We can now finish our whole analysis of the pricing of factors. We remember that in our last example it was profitable for our farmers to buy tractors, rather than land or labor. Now we must suppose that many

*The diagram does not show a very important difference in *scale*. One inch along the horizontal axis of the industry diagram on the left may represent 100,000 units. The same inch along the firm's horizontal axis would then stand for only a few hundred units.

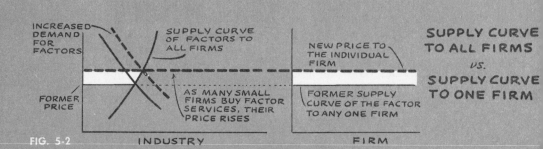

FIG. 5-2

INCREASED DEMAND FOR FACTORS

SUPPLY CURVE OF FACTORS TO ALL FIRMS

NEW PRICE TO THE INDIVIDUAL FIRM

SUPPLY CURVE TO ALL FIRMS
vs.
SUPPLY CURVE TO ONE FIRM

FORMER PRICE

AS MANY SMALL FIRMS BUY FACTOR SERVICES, THEIR PRICE RISES

FORMER SUPPLY CURVE OF THE FACTOR TO ANY ONE FIRM

INDUSTRY   FIRM

farmers, finding themselves in a similar situation, all bid for tractors. The result, of course, is that tractor prices will rise. How far? Suppose they went from $2,000 to $2,300. Assuming that the marginal productivity of the tractor in use has not changed, it will now cost the farmer $2,300 to get the $2,500 of revenue from an additional tractor. This is a return of $1.09 on a dollar's outlay. At that return, tractors are no longer the best factor buy, but land is. Hence our farmers will begin bidding for land instead of tractors.

Suppose that as a result of their bids, acreage rentals rise from $500 to $550. Now for a dollar spent on land a farmer will no longer get back $1.20, but only $1.09, or the same as the return on capital. Thereupon, our farmers turn their factor bids toward labor, which has changed from the worst to the best buy on the factor market. Suppose as a result of general bidding for labor, the wage rises from $4,500 to $4,900. Now a dollar spent for labor will also bring $1.09 in return. At this point, one factor is as advantageous as another.

The bidding will continue, of course, because *any* factor added will still bring a net return to the farmer. But now the competition for factors will cause *all* their prices to rise (maintaining the same proportion to one another) until the increasing expense of all factors, or their diminishing physical productivity, finally brings the bidding process to a halt.

But now see what has happened:

1. *All factors will be sought as long as their marginal cost is less than their marginal revenue.* Therefore, factors will be bid for until their remuneration approaches the revenue they bring the firm. In a competitive market such as we have described, there can be no "exploitation" — that is, no factor can receive less than the value of output for which its physical productivity is responsible.

2. *All factors will be priced in relation to one another, so that their rewards will mirror their respective marginal productivities.* The prices of the services of land, labor, and capital, or of different grades of each, will be exactly proportional to the marginal contribution each makes to output.

3. *As firms seek to equalize factor yields, they are also combining factors in the most efficient possible way.* Later we shall see that this brings consumers the benefit of the lowest possible prices. Now we can also see that by maximizing factor productivity, it brings about the highest possible factor prices, or remunerations.

The market solution to distribution

We can begin to grasp the remarkable nature of the market as a system for solving the problems of distribution, at least in the world of atomistic competition we have so far studied. But our analysis also reveals a disturbing fact. It is that attempts to interfere with the market mechanism for pricing factors may bring unexpected — and unwanted —

effects. Take for example the problem of low-priced labor. Suppose the government decided tomorrow to eliminate all low-paid work by legislating a minimum wage of $100 a week (or suppose that trade unions accomplished the same thing through bargaining).

What would be the result? As the price of low-paid labor rises, the differential in pay that compensated for its lower productivity is removed. The unavoidable consequence is that entrepreneurs will swing their factor demand toward other factors — land, capital, or high-priced labor — because a dollar of expenditure will now bring them a larger return from these factors. Hence the result of the minimum wage is very likely to bring unemployment to the very persons it was designed to help!

How *much* unemployment depends on how "substitutable" is the factor in question. Suppose the new minimum wage affects the pay of grocery boys. Grocers will try to use trucks to make deliveries wherever possible instead of sending boys on bicycles, or they will simply eliminate some deliveries. If it is possible to persuade customers to carry their own groceries, or if it is not too expensive to deliver groceries by truck, many delivery boys will be let go. In the latter case, in more technical terms, if capital can be substituted for labor, a slight rise in the price of labor will mean a considerable swing from labor-using to relatively capital-using techniques. In that case, delivery boys' aggregate incomes are likely to suffer.

If, on the other hand, grocers find that they can't replace the delivery boy system, they will be forced to retain most of the boys and to pay them higher wages. As a result, grocery prices will rise somewhat, and the quantity of groceries demanded will decrease — how much or little depending on the price-elasticity of demand for groceries. If demand is very elastic, sales will fall off sharply, and many delivery boys will be fired because there is no need for them. If enough are fired, the income of the whole group may even fall. On the other hand, if demand is inelastic, grocery sales will remain relatively unchanged, few delivery boys will be let go, and their incomes as a whole will rise.

Thus the effect of setting floors under factor prices is difficult to predict insofar as its effect on *incomes* is concerned. Here everything depends on the technical ease of substituting other factors in place of the one whose price has been pushed up, and on the elasticities of demand for the final good or service itself. But the effect on *employment* must always be adverse, although again its extent will hinge on substitutability and elasticities of demand for final products.

Hence the efforts of government authorities or of trade unions to raise wages can backfire and actually reduce the incomes as well as the employment of those affected. To point this out is not to preach against such efforts. There are powerful arguments of social justice that favor some interventions into the market process. But one must not overlook the fact that interventions to "remedy" the rewards of the market will invariably bring their side effects. A thoughtful social policy will anticipate these effects and will not intervene into the market without plans for coping with the repercussions that are apt to ensue.

Marginal productivity and social justice

But why interfere in the market process at all? Is not the market's solution to the problem of distribution a just and equitable one? If A is twice as productive as B, should he not be paid twice as much?

There are two important caveats before we accept this deceptively attractive proposition. First, the market will not price factors according to their marginal productivities if there are impediments to the free movement of factors within society. The same barriers that we discovered in our last chapter, where demand originated with consumers rather than with business firms, distort the entrepreneurial determination of income as they do the direct pricing factors. Tariffs or union barriers or patent restrictions, immobilities due to geographical location or lack of education—all impair the achievement of the solution that microtheory promises. In addition, in the real world, where firms are by no means always the small competitive units we have dealt with, the buyer of factors may be able to pay them less than their marginal productivity warrants, because there are no competitive firms to bid factors away. Hence, as was the case previously, we must not make the serious error of confusing the distribution of incomes in the real world with that of an ideal market, or commit the error of defending those incomes on the basis of theoretical premises that may not fit the case.

Second, even if all factors were remunerated in proportion to their productivities, it does not follow that the resulting levels of compensation would be "just." Even if one man is twice as productive as another, there is no inherent reason why he "should" be compensated twice as highly. Should a young worker, who is unmarried, make more money than an older one with a large family? Nor is there any inherent reason that, because a dollar's worth of land or capital makes a larger contribution to output than a dollar's worth of labor, the *owners* of those resources should therefore receive a compensation as large as the marginal revenue product of "their" resources. As John Stuart Mill wrote in a famous passage in his *Principles of Economics* in 1848:

The things are there; mankind individually or collectively can do with them as they please. They can place them at the disposal of whomsoever they please, and on whatever terms. The distribution of wealth . . . depends on the laws and customs of society. The rules by which it is determined are what the opinions and feelings of the ruling portion of the community make them, and are very different in different ages and countries, and might be still more different, if mankind so chose.

Thus the market solution must be judged on its *efficacy*, not on its "intrinsic" merits. The rewards meted out by the market serve a purpose — to maintain the efficiency of the market system — but we should not confuse their functional merits with their moral worth. This is particularly pertinent to a society of considerable affluence in which the sheer necessity for efficiency of output becomes a matter of less pressing moment and in which, accordingly, other noneconomic standards can be allowed to play a more prominent role in the establishment of the community's goals.

Summary

1. The study of the firm concentrates initially on the small enterprise. It assumes that such enterprises act intelligently and rationally and that they *try to maximize their profits in the short run*.
2. In all enterprises there is a *minimum size* or scale necessary for effective competition. This size is essentially determined by technology.
3. The choice of the amounts of the remaining factors to be added will be determined by their *profitability*.
4. Their profitability in turn will depend to an important degree on their *productivity*. This leads to the discovery that as we add any factor to a fixed supply of other factors *its marginal productivity changes*. Initially it rises, and we enjoy increasing average returns. Subsequently it begins to decline, and the average drops. At this point we enter the stage of diminishing average returns.
5. The *law of diminishing returns* (or *variable proportions*) applies to any factor, provided that we hold the amounts of the other factors fixed. It is entirely a natural phenomenon, not a behavioral one.
6. Marginal productivity is a critical element in determining the *marginal revenue* we can expect from hiring a factor. This marginal revenue will then be compared with marginal cost, to determine whether the unit of the factor is profitable.
7. The addition of factors is made by *comparing the returns from alternative factor mixes*. The factor yielding the highest return per dollar will be the factor that is hired.
8. *The process of many entrepreneurs bidding for the most profitable factor will raise its price.* Any single entrepreneur can bid for a factor without affecting its price; but when all firms bid for the same factor, its price rises.
9. This bidding process will eventually *equalize the return* to be had among all factors. The result is threefold:
   • *All factors will be sought as long as their marginal cost is less than their marginal revenue;* i.e., there will be no exploitation.
   • *All factors will be priced relative to one another in proportion to their marginal productivities.*
   • *Factors will be combined in the most efficient possible way.*

10. *If any factor price is "artificially" raised, its employment must be reduced* because other factors will now be relatively cheaper. Whether or not the more expensive factor suffers a fall in income depends on the technical possibilities of substitution and on the elasticity of demand for the end product.

11. The pricing of factors according to their respective marginal productivities is an *efficient but not necessarily "just" solution* to the problem of distribution.

Questions

1. Suppose that you were about to open a small business — say a drugstore. What do you think would be the factor that was critical in determining the scale of your operation? Name businesses in which land, labor, and capital, respectively, would play this limiting role.

2. Once you had decided on your scale, what consideration would be uppermost in your mind when you were deciding how much of the other two factors to hire? What is the cardinal rule you would have to bear in mind in deciding if a unit of a factor would or would not pay its way?

3. One thing that would affect your decision to hire or not to hire a factor would be the amount of physical increase in output it would yield. What is the generalization we make about the change in output associated with combining more and more of one factor to a fixed combination of others. Is this generalization based on behavior? State the law of variable proportions as carefully as you can.

4. What is meant by marginal productivity? What is its relation to average productivity? Suppose that you were considering the increase in your drug sales that would result from adding square feet of space. Draw up a schedule showing that the addition of square footage (in units of 100 sq ft) would at first yield increasing returns (dollars of sales) and then diminishing returns.

5. Suppose that a manufacturer had the following information for a given plant and number of men:

Number of machines	Total output (units)
1	100
2	250
3	450
4	600
5	710
6	750
7	775
8	780

What would be the marginal productivity of each successive machine? The average productivity from using additional machines? When would diminishing *marginal* productivity set in? Diminishing *average* productivity?

6. Why must we hold the other factors constant to derive the law of variable proportions?

7. Suppose that each machine in our example above cost $1,000 and that each unit of output sold for $10. How many machines would it be most profitable to hire? (Figure out the marginal revenue and marginal cost for each machine added.)

8. What would be the most profitable number to have if the cost of the machine rose to $1,500? If the price per unit of sales fell to $9?

9. Suppose that our manufacturer found he had the following alternatives:
   - He could spend $1,000 on a machine that would add 115 units to sales (each unit selling at $10).
   - He could spend $5,000 to hire a new man who would increase output by 510 units.
   - He could rent new space for $10,000 that would make possible an increase in output of 1,100 units.

   How would he know which was the best factor to hire? Would he have to begin by asking what is his dollar return per dollar of cost in each case? What is this in the case of the machine? The new man? The land? Which is the best buy?

10. If one manufacturer in a competitive market adds to his factor inputs, will that affect their price? What happens when all manufacturers bid for the same factor? In the example above, which factor will be bid for? What will happen to its price? What will then be the "best buy"? What will happen to *its* price? What will be the final output of the bidding?

11. In the end, what will be the relation between the prices of factors? Will it be proportional to their costs? To their average outputs? To their marginal productivities? Explain carefully which is correct.

12. How do we know that there will be no "exploitation" of factors in a competitive market?

13. Suppose that the manufacturers of a certain kind of machinery got together (illegally) and agreed to keep its price above the level that would be set in a competitive market. What would happen to the number of machines they sold? What would we have to know before we could predict the effect on their total incomes?

14. By and large, do you think the market is a just allocator of incomes? If not, why not; and what would you suggest to improve it?

6

The equilibrium
of the firm

We have reached the last step in our analysis of the circular flow in the marketplace. We have learned how households create a demand for goods and services by spending their incomes in the market, and we have had a glimpse of the supply of goods and services coming to meet their demand. Then we have followed those selfsame householders in their role as factors of production, and we have discovered how the incomes they had spent were earned by selling their services to other individuals and to firms.

Now it remains only to close the circuit. We must complete the circular flow inside the firm itself: watch the enterprise receive revenues from the market and transfer them to the pockets of its factors of production. At the same time, we can complete our picture of how the firm, which is the active pump of the circular flow, serves both as an agency of the market system and as an organization in search of its own private ends.

Inside the firm: fixed and variable cost

This will require us once again to put ourselves in the shoes of an imaginary entrepreneur. Since we have already become familiar with the firm's calculations in regard to buying factor services, let us begin our inquiry into the firm by extending our knowledge into a full appreciation of what the cost problem looks like to the entrepreneur.

We know that a firm's total costs must rise as it hires additional factors. Yet if we put ourselves in a businessman's position, we can see that our total costs are unlikely to rise as fast as our additional factor costs, because there are some costs of production that will not be affected by an increase in factor input. Real estate taxes, for example, will remain unchanged if we hire one man or 100—so long as we do not acquire additional land. The depreciation cost of machinery will not be affected by additions to land or labor. Rent will be unchanged, unless the premises are expanded. The cost of electric light will not vary appreciably despite additions to labor or machinery. Neither will the salary of the president. *Thus some costs, determined by legal contract or by usage or by the unchanging use of one factor, do not vary with output. We call these fixed costs.*

In sharp contrast with fixed costs is another kind of cost that does vary directly with output. Here are most factor costs, for generally we vary inputs of labor and capital (and sometimes land) every time we seek a new level of production. To increase output almost always requires the payment of more wages and the employment of more capital (if only in the form of inventories) and sometimes the rental of more space. *We call all costs that vary with output variable costs.*

Cost per unit

Thus, as a manufacturer (or a farmer or a storekeeper) expands his output, typically his total costs rise because his variable costs are going up, but they do not rise as fast as his variable costs, because his fixed costs are set. But it is not easy to visualize this upward rising curve of total costs. Hence businessmen and economists alike convert the figures for total cost into *unit costs,* by dividing the total by the number of units of goods produced. This results, of course, in a figure for the *average cost per unit of output.* We shall see that this gives us a very useful way of figuring what happens to costs as output expands.

There is certainly no difficulty in picturing what happens to fixed costs per unit of output as output rises. By definition, they must fall. Suppose our manufacturer has fixed costs (rent and certain indirect taxes and depreciation and "overhead") of $50,000 a year. If he produces 50,000 units of his product per year, each unit will have to bear $1 of fixed costs as its share. If output rises to 100,000 units, the unit share of fixed costs will shrink to 50¢. At 500,000 units it would be a dime. Thus a curve of fixed costs per unit of output would look like Fig. 6-1.

What about variable costs per unit? Here the situation is more complex, for it depends directly on the analysis of the productivity curve we discussed in our last chapter. Hence, let us first set up a schedule of output for our manufacturer, showing how the total numbers of units he produces will rise at first rapidly, then more slowly, as factor inputs change. Although this will be true, as we know, for all factors, let us simplify things by following only the case of labor.

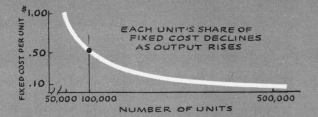

EACH UNIT'S SHARE OF
FIXED COST DECLINES
AS OUTPUT RISES

PROFILE OF
FIXED COSTS
PER UNIT

FIG. 6-1

**TABLE
6 • 1**

Number of men	Total output	Marginal product
10	50,000	50,000
11	130,000	80,000
12	230,000	100,000
13	320,000	90,000
14	380,000	60,000
15	400,000	20,000
16	410,000	10,000

To convert this schedule of physical productivity into a unit cost figure, we must do two things: (1) we need to know the cost of the factor in question, so that we can calculate total variable cost for each level of output, and (2) we must then divide the total variable cost by the number of units to get average variable cost per unit. Here are the figures (assuming that the going wage is $5,000).

**TABLE
6 • 2**

Number of men	Total variable cost	Total output (units)	Average variable cost per unit
10	$50,000	50,000	$1.00
11	55,000	130,000	.42
12	60,000	230,000	.26
13	65,000	320,000	.20
14	70,000	380,000	.18
15	75,000	400,000	.19
16	80,000	410,000	.20

Notice that average variable costs per unit decline at first and thereafter rise. The reason is by now clear enough. Variable cost increases by a set amount — $5,000 per man — as factors are added. Output, however, obeys the law of variable proportions, increasing rapidly at first and then displaying diminishing returns. It stands to reason, then, that the variable cost *per unit* of output will be falling as long as output is growing faster than costs, and that it will begin to rise as soon as additions to output start to get smaller.

87

If we graph the typical variable cost curve per unit of output, it will be the dish-shaped or U-shaped profile that Fig. 6-2 shows.

We can now set up a complete cost schedule for our enterprise by combining fixed and variable costs.

TABLE 6 • 3

Number of men	Total cost ($50,000 fixed cost+ $5,000 per man	Output (units)	Average cost per unit (total cost ÷ output)	Marginal cost per unit (change in total cost ÷ change in output
10	$100,000	50,000	$2.00	$ –
11	105,000	130,000	.74	.06
12	110,000	230,000	.48	.05
13	115,000	320,000	.40	.06
14	120,000	380,000	.32	.08
15	125,000	400,000	.31	.25
16	130,000	410,000	.32	.50

If we graph the last two columns of figures—average and marginal cost per unit—we get the very important diagram in Fig. 6-3.

The cost profile

We have reached the end of our cost calculations, and it will help to take stock of what we have done. Actually, despite all the figures and diagrams, the procedure has been quite simple.

1. We began by seeing what would happen to our *fixed costs* per unit as we expanded output. Since fixed costs, by their nature, do not increase as production increases, the amount of fixed cost that had to be charged to each unit of output fell sharply as output rose.

2. Next we calculated the *variable costs* that would have to be borne by each unit as output increased. Here the critical process at work was the law of variable proportions. As the marginal productivity of factors increased, variable cost per unit fell. But when the inevitable stage of diminishing returns set in, variable costs per unit had to rise.

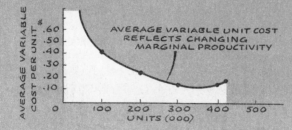

AVERAGE VARIABLE UNIT COST REFLECTS CHANGING MARGINAL PRODUCTIVITY

PROFILE OF CHANGING VARIABLE COSTS PER UNIT

FIG. 6-2

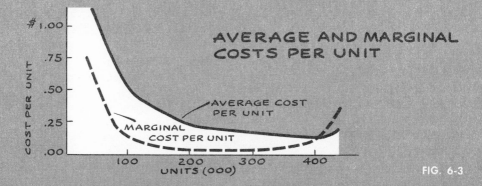

AVERAGE AND MARGINAL COSTS PER UNIT

FIG. 6-3

3. Adding together fixed and variable costs, we obtained the *total unit cost* of output. Like the variable cost curve, average total unit costs are dish-shaped, reflecting the diminishing marginal productivity of factors as output grows.

4. Finally, we show the changing *marginal cost per unit*—the increase in total costs divided by the increase in output. As before, it is the changing marginal costs that the entrepreneur actually experiences when he alters output. It is the increase at the margin that changes his total cost, and which therefore determines his average cost.

Average and marginal costs

Actually, the cost profile that we have worked out would be known by any businessman whether he had ever studied microeconomics or not. Whenever a firm starts producing, its average cost per unit of output is very high. A General Motors plant turning out only a few hundred cars a year would have astronomical costs per automobile.

But as output increases, unit costs come down steadily, partly because overhead (fixed costs) is now spread over more units, partly because the factors are used at much greater efficiency. Finally, after some point of maximum factor efficiency, average unit costs begin to mount. Even though overhead continues to decline, it is now so small a fraction of cost per unit that its further decline does not count for much, while the rising inefficiency of factors pushes up variable cost per unit steadily. If General Motors tries to jam more cars through a plant than it is designed to take, the cost per auto will again begin to soar.

So much for the average cost per unit. By directing our attention to the *changes* that occur in total cost and total output every time we alter the number of factors we engage, the marginal cost curve per unit simply tells us why all this is happening. In other words, as our plant first moves into high gear, the cars we add to the line (the marginal output) will cost considerably less than the average of all cars processed previously; later, when diminishing returns begins to work against us, we would expect the added (marginal) cars to be high-cost cars, higher in cost than the average of all cars built so far.

Since the cost of marginal output always "leads" the cost of average output in this way, we can understand an important relationship that the marginal and average curves always bear to one another. *The marginal cost curve always cuts the average cost curve at the lowest point of the latter.*

Why? Because as long as the additional cars are cheaper than the average of all cars, their production must be *reducing* average cost—that is, as long as the marginal cost curve is lower than the average cost curve, the average cost curve must be falling. Conversely, as soon as additional output is more expensive than the average for all previous output, that additional production must *raise* average costs—again, (look at the previous diagram) as soon as marginal cost is above average cost, average cost must begin to rise. Hence it follows that the *MC* (marginal cost) curve must cross the *AC* (average cost) curve at the minimum point of the latter. This relationship has nothing to do with economics, as such, but with simple logic, as Fig. 6-4 may elucidate.

From cost to revenue

The cost profile gives us a clear picture of what happens to unit costs as our firm hires additional factors. But that is only half the information we need to understand how a firm operates with one foot in the factor market and the other in the market for goods. Now we need a comparable profile of what happens to revenues as the firm sells the output its factors have made for it.

This brings us over from supply to demand—from dealing with factors who are selling their services, back to householders who are buying goods. What the entrepreneur wants to know is whether "the market" will buy his goods and if so, at just what price it will buy them. In other words, he wants to know the demand curve for his particular output. If he knows that, he can easily figure what his revenues will be.

What does the demand curve look like for a small competitive firm? Let us take the case of our manufacturer, with whose costs we are now familiar, and assume that the "units" he is making are simple metal stampings of which several million are sold each year. Our manufacturer knows two things about the market for those stampings. First, he knows that there is a "going" price for stampings (which we will say is 40¢)

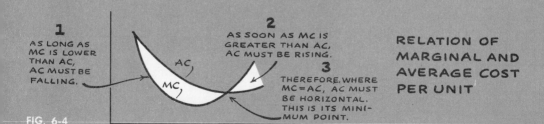

1
AS LONG AS MC IS LOWER THAN AC, AC MUST BE FALLING.

2
AS SOON AS MC IS GREATER THAN AC, AC MUST BE RISING.

3
THEREFORE, WHERE MC=AC, AC MUST BE HORIZONTAL. THIS IS ITS MINIMUM POINT.

AC

MC

RELATION OF MARGINAL AND AVERAGE COST PER UNIT

FIG. 6-4

that is established by "the market." Second, he knows that he can personally sell all the stampings he can make at the going price without altering that price by so much as a penny—that "the market" will not be affected whether he closes down his shop entirely or whether he sells every last stamping he can afford to make at the price the market offers.

What our manufacturer knows in his bones, we can translate into economics. The price of any commodity is set in the goods market by the interplay of supply and demand. Our firm is one of the many suppliers whose willingness and ability to sell at different prices (which are, of course, largely determined by their costs) makes up the supply curve. The demand curve for the commodity is familiar to us as the expression of the consumers' willingness and ability to buy.

But now we can also see that as far as the output of any *one* small firm is concerned, the demand for *its* output is a horizontal line—that there is an "infinite" willingness to buy its product, provided it can be supplied at the going price.* The output of any one seller, in other words, is too small to affect the equilibrium price for the market as a whole.

Thus the competitive firm operates between two horizontal curves. On the supply side it faces a perfectly elastic supply of factors, meaning that it can hire all the factors it wishes without changing prices an iota in the factor market. On the demand side it also faces a perfectly elastic curve, meaning that it can sell as much as it can produce without any perceptible price effect here, either. The firm is thus squeezed between two forces that it is powerless to change. As a result, it must devote all its energies to those parts of the market process that are in its control—the efficient combining of factors to minimize its costs, and the selection of the most profitable scale and line of output.

Average and marginal revenue

Facing a known demand curve, our manufacturer can now calculate his revenues. He will take in an amount determined by his total unit output multiplied by the price of each unit. And since, with a horizontal demand curve, the price of each unit will be exactly the same price as the previous one, the marginal revenue of each unit sold—that is the additional amount it will bring in—will be unchanged no matter how much is sold by the firm. If the selling price is 40¢, then the marginal revenue per unit will be 40¢. As a result, average revenue per unit will also be 40¢. The schedules of revenue will look like the table on the following page.

*Why cannot, then, an ambitious firm make an "infinite" profit by expanding its sales to match demand? The shape of its cost curve gives the answer. As factor productivity declined, marginal costs would soon be above selling price.

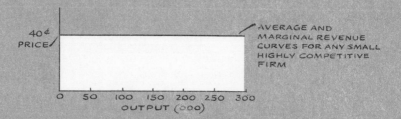

FIG. 6-5

Output (units)	Price per unit	Marginal revenue per unit	Total revenue	Avg. revenue per unit
50,000	.40	.40	$ 20,000	.40
100,000	.40	.40	40,000	.40
150,000	.40	.40	60,000	.40
200,000	.40	.40	80,000	.40
250,000	.40	.40	100,000	.40
300,000	.40	.40	120,000	.40

We can see that a graph of the average and marginal costs curves for this (or any) small, highly competitive firm would look like Fig. 6-5.

/ Marginal revenue and marginal cost

Now we have all the information we want. We have a cost profile that tells us what happens to unit costs as we hire or fire factors. We have a revenue profile that tells us what happens to unit revenues as we do the same. It remains only to put the two together to discover just how much output the firm should make to maximize its profits.

We can do this very simply by superimposing the revenue diagram on top of the cost diagram. The point where the marginal revenue and the marginal cost curves meet should indicate exactly what the most profitable output will be. We see this in Fig. 25-6.

Why is this the point of best possible output? Because another unit of output—as we can see by looking at the two curves—will cost more than it brings in, while a unit less of output would deprive him of the additional net revenue that another unit of output could bring.

What is the total amount of profit our firm makes at this level of output? That is very difficult to tell from the diagram above, since it is hard to figure out what total cost is. But with the addition of our familiar curve of average costs per unit, we can tell at a glance. Average costs, as we know, are nothing but total costs reduced to a per-unit basis. So are average revenues. Hence, *if we compare the average unit revenue and cost curves at any point, they will tell us at a glance what total revenues and costs look like at that point.*

Figure 6-7 reveals what our situation is at the point of optimum

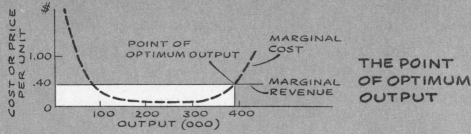

output. (This time we generalize the diagram rather than putting it into the specific terms of our illustrative firm.)

The diagram shows several things. First, as before, it indicates our most profitable output as the amount *OA* – the output indicated by the point *X,* where the marginal revenue and marginal cost curves meet. Second, it shows us that at output *OA*, our *average cost* is *OC (= AB)* and our *average revenue* is *OD (= AX)*, the same as our marginal revenue, since the demand curve for the firm is horizontal. Our profit on the *average* unit of output must therefore be *CD (= BX)*, the difference between average costs and average revenues at this point. The *total* profit is therefore the rectangle *CDXB*, which is the average profit per unit (*CD*) times the number of units.

The firm and the industry

Our firm is now in equilibrium. It is making about 390,000 stampings (if you will look up at Fig. 6-6, you will see that our firm's marginal costs turn up very sharply after 380,000 units), at an average cost of something under 31¢ and selling them for 40¢. Its profit is roughly $39,000.* This is as much money as our firm can make, given the price for its product and the going prices of factors.

However satisfactory from the point of view of the firm, this is not yet a satisfactory stopping point from the point of view of the system as a whole. If our firm is typical of the metal stamping industry, then small firms throughout this line of business are making profits comparable to ours. Unhappily for them, there are numerous businesses in other lines

---

*We will have more to say about profit later. At this juncture, it should be said only that profit is what is left *after* all factors have been paid, including whatever wages are due to management.

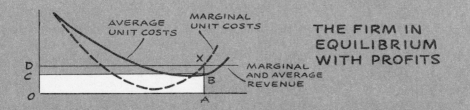

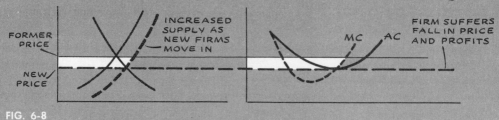

FIG. 6-8

of endeavor that do not make $39,000 of clear profit. *Hence entrepreneurs in these lines will now begin to move into our profitable industry.*

Perhaps we can anticipate what will now happen. Our firm is now going to experience the same "mysterious" change in prices that we have already witnessed in the factor market, when many firms altered their demands for land or labor or capital and the prices of these factor services changed accordingly. Only this time, it is the price of goods that will change, not that of factors. For the influx of entrepreneurs from other areas will move the industry supply curve to the right and thereby reduce the going price. As it falls, our own business will experience a disconcerting fall in the price for its goods which it is powerless to stop. We can see the process in Fig. 6-8.

How long will this influx of firms continue? Suppose that it continues until price falls *below* the average cost curve of our representative firm. Now its position looks like Fig. 6-9. Output will still be set where *MC = MR,* but now the average cost curve is above the average revenue curve at this point. The unavoidable result is a loss for the firm, as the diagram shows.

What will happen? Clearly, we need a reverse adjustment process — an exodus of firms into greener pastures, so that the supply curve for our industry can move to the left, bringing higher prices for all producers. This may not be a rapid process, but eventually depreciation and the withdrawal of producers should bring about the necessary adjustment, shown in Fig. 6-10.*

---

*There is an interesting reason for this slowness. A firm can suffer losses for quite a while, as long as its revenues are high enough to pay its variable costs and a little more. In that case, it can meet some of its fixed costs from its operating income. If it shut down entirely, *its fixed costs would continue.* Thus it will lose less money if it continues to produce — provided always that its revenues meet its variable costs in full and cover part, if

THE FIRM SUFFERING A LOSS

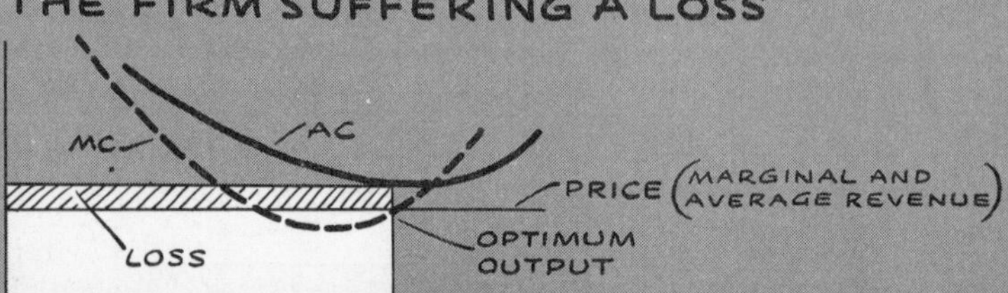

FIG. 6-9

Long-run equilibrium

Finally we reach a point of equilibrium both for the firm and the industry (or the system as a whole). It looks, of course, like Fig. 6-11.

Note that this position of equilibrium has two characteristics.

1. *Marginal cost equals marginal revenue,* so there is no incentive for the individual entrepreneur to alter his own output.
2. *Average cost equals average revenue* (or price), so there is no incentive for firms to enter or leave the industry.

Thus we can state the conditions for the equilibrium resting point of our firm and industry as being a four-way equality:

$$P = MR = MC = AC$$

Profits and equilibrium

We have reached an equilibrium both for the firm and for the industry, but it is certainly an uncomfortable one for ourselves as typical manufacturers. For in the final resting point of the firm, it is clear that *profits have been totally eliminated.* Is this a realistic assumption?

The question forces us to confront the slippery question of what "profits" are. By definition, they are not returns to factors, for these payments have already been made by the firm—including all payments made to entrepreneurs for the full value of their contribution to output.*

---

not all, of its fixed expenses. Eventually, of course, such a firm will go bankrupt, for it will be spending more than it is taking in. But it will go bankrupt more quickly if it stops producing altogether, for then it could pay none of its fixed costs! Hence it will go on producing, thereby delaying the needed market adjustment.

*To put it differently, we do not include in the term *profit* any revenues the firm *must* have to stay in business. An accountant, examining the books of a marginal firm in an industry, might find that there was a small bookkeeping profit. But an economist, looking at these revenues, would not call this sum a true economic profit if it were necessary to maintain the firm (or its entrepreneur) in operation. We should note as well that profits are usually figured as a return on the capital invested in a firm, and not as a return on each unit sold. It is simpler for our purposes, however, (and it does no violence to the argument) to talk of profits in relation to output (= sales) rather than as a return on investment.

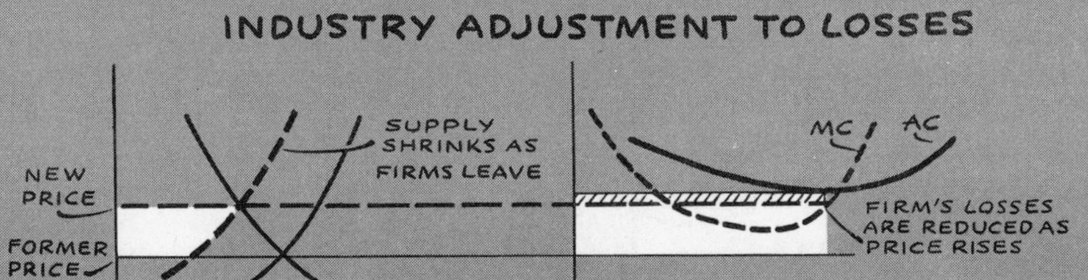

INDUSTRY ADJUSTMENT TO LOSSES

SUPPLY SHRINKS AS FIRMS LEAVE

NEW PRICE

FORMER PRICE

MC   AC

FIRM'S LOSSES ARE REDUCED AS PRICE RISES

FIG. 6-10

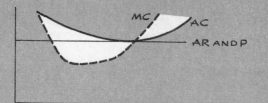

FIG. 6-11

THE MARGINAL FIRM
IN EQUILIBRIUM
WITH NO PROFIT

What are profits, then? There have been numerous attempts to define them as the return for risk, or for innovation, and so on. But however we describe them, we are driven to the conclusion that in a "perfect" competitive market, the forces of competition would indeed press toward zero the returns of the *marginal* firms in all industries, so that the cost and revenue profile of the last firms able to remain alive in each industry would look like our diagram.

Note, however, that these are marginal firms. Here is a clue to how profits can exist even in a highly competitive situation. In Fig. 6-12, we show the supply curve of an industry, broken down into the individual supply curves of its constituent firms. Some of these firms, by virtue of superior location, or access to supplies, or managerial skills will be lower-cost producers than others. When the industry price is finally established, they will be the beneficiaries of the difference between the going price (which reduces the profits of the marginal firm to zero) and the lower unit costs attributable to their superior efficiency.

Really, these intramarginal profits are *quasi rents*. That is, they result from scarcities—of location, or managerial talents, or whatever—that earn a high return. If, through a fall in price, any one of these firms were suddenly put at the margin of production, it would continue to produce, fully covering its costs, but earning no profits. Even without a fall in price, we would expect intramarginal rents to diminish over time, owing to factor mobility. Badly located firms will pick up and move, or newcomers will locate favorably and thereby displace a firm at the margin. Managerial skills will be learned elsewhere or hired. Thus in the long run, we must expect the *tendency* in a fully competitive market to be a constant pressure toward lower prices, and thus toward the elimination of quasi rents.

Long and short run

We have seen how the market makes it necessary for firms to produce goods at the lowest points along their average unit cost curves and to

DEMAND   MARGINAL FIRM,
          ZERO PROFIT

GOING
PRICE   INTRAMARGINAL
             PROFITABLE
             FIRMS

INTRAMARGINAL
PROFITS

FIG. 6-12

sell those goods at prices that will yield no profit to the least efficient firm in the industry. Yet there is one last adjustment process to consider. In all our investigations into the firm's operations, we have hitherto taken for granted that the *scale of output* would remain unchanged. As a result, all of our adjustments have involved us in moving back and forth along a cost curve that was basically set in place by one or more limiting factors.

This may be accurate enough in the short run, when most firms are circumscribed by a given size of plant, but it certainly does not describe the long run. A firm can usually enlarge its scale of plant; and as the scale increases, it is often possible to realize additional savings in cost, as a result of still finer specialization of the production process. If our expanding firm confines its growth to a single plant, the cost curves of these successive scales of output are apt to look like Fig. 6-13.

If we connect the successive short-run cost curves attributable to various scales of output, we get a *long-run average unit cost curve* shown in the heavy line below. We have laready explained that its initial downward slope is due to savings that size continues to bring in the utilization of factors. The extent to which a firm will be able to realize these so-called *economies of scale* depends mainly on the technological possibilities in its industry. For example, note that the development of mass production in the late nineteenth century brought about a change in many industries from atomistic competition to the domination of a few, very large-scale producers.

Our diagram shows, however, that economies of scale do not go on forever. At some point—again determined by technology—the limits of efficient plant operation are reached. A sprawling enterprise begins to

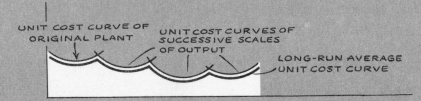

LONG-RUN COST CURVE

UNIT COST CURVE OF
ORIGINAL PLANT   UNIT COST CURVES OF
                  SUCCESSIVE SCALES
                  OF OUTPUT
                          LONG-RUN AVERAGE
                          UNIT COST CURVE

FIG. 6-13

stretch the coordinating powers of management too thin. *Diseconomies of scale* enter, and the long-run unit cost curve again begins to mount.*

There is still, however, another way in which our firm's long-run costs can be altered. Together with all of its competitors it may be subject to *increasing or decreasing costs for the industry as a whole.*

The source of these changes in cost do not lie within the firm, in the relative efficiency of various factor mixes. Rather, they are changes thrust upon the firm — for better or worse — by the interaction of the growing industry of which it is a part and the economy as a whole. A new industry, for example, by its very expansion may bring into being satellite firms that provide some of its necessary inputs; and as the main new industry grows, the satellites also expand and thereby realize economies of scale that will benefit the main industry itself. The automobile industry was surely an instance of such long-run falling costs (for a long period, at least) resulting from the economies of scale enjoyed by makers of tires, makers of batteries and other equipment. In turn, the rise of low-cost trucking brought "external economies" to many other industries.

Industries may also experience long-run rising costs if their expansion pushes them up against factor scarcity of a stubbornly inelastic kind. Extractive industries, for example, may be forced to use progressively less-accessible mineral deposits; or agricultural industries may be forced to use progressively less-fertile or less-conveniently located land. Such industries would experience a gradual rise in unit costs as their output increased.

Are most industries the beneficiaries of decreasing cost or the victims of increasing cost? Empirical studies seem to suggest that save for youthful, growing industries, and for the special case of extractive ones, most industries enjoy a middle position of roughly constant long-run unit costs, at least over a considerable period of time. That is, for most industries it is probably accurate to state that the so-called *external*

---

*Note that these long-run cost curves apply to individual *plants*. What about a firm that pushes each plant to its optimum size and then adds a new plant, or a firm that diversifies its efforts among many different kinds of businesses? Does it also face a long-run, upward sloping cost curve, owing perhaps to eventual diseconomies of management? We really do not know the answer. To hazard an unsubstantiated guess, it may well be that the new technology of information retrieval has so increased the efficiency of management that the economically effective size of multiplant or diversified plants is today extremely large. For all practical purposes, the management cost curve is probably horizontal or perhaps even falling.

economies or *diseconomies* are much less important than internal economies or diseconomies.

The competitive environment

Our consideration of the forces bearing on long-run costs brings our discussion of the firm to an end. We have seen how the firm has closed the circular flow by transforming its receipts from householders into payments to its factors, and we have simultaneously watched as it performed its social function of combining factors as efficiently as possible in the course of pursuing its short-run profits.

Now we must ask a question that has surely occurred to the reader. Does the world really behave as microtheory has portrayed it? Do firms really equate marginal costs and revenues or balance the advantages of one factor versus another with the fine precision that our model has indicated? That is not a question we can fully answer until our next chapter. But we already know one condition that must be fulfilled if firms are to behave as we have pictured them. This is the condition of "pure" competition to which we have already referred as the environment we would take for granted during our initial microeconomic investigations. Now is the time to look carefully into exactly what the term means.

Pure competition defined

In general, when economists use the term *pure competition,* they imply three necessary attributes of the market situation:

1. *Large numbers of marketers*

Unless there are numerous buyers and sellers facing one another across the market and jostling one another on each side of it, the competitive process will not fully work itself out. When the number of marketers is few (whether as buyers or sellers) the vying among them that gives competition its resistless force is apt to be muted or even lacking entirely. As the extreme case of this we have outright *collusion,* in which a few buyers or sellers agree to bid only at one low price or to offer only at one high price. But even when collusion is absent, fewness of buyers or sellers will lead, as we shall see in our next chapter, to results that are considerably at variance with those of the competitive process we have assumed.

How many buyers or sellers does it take to make a fully competitive market? There is no clear-cut answer. The critical number is reached when no firm, by varying its scale of output, is able to affect the price of the factors it buys or the product it sells. We have pictured this condition in terms of the horizontal factor supply and market demand curves that present the purely competitive firm with the unalterable data of factor and goods prices to which it must accommodate itself. *Thus under conditions of pure competition, the only thing the firm can control is its scale of output and the mix of factors it uses; all prices are beyond its power to influence.*

2. *Ease of entry into, and exit out of industries*

A second prerequisite for so-called pure competition is a condition that we have already relied upon frequently in discussing the operation of the market. *This is the ability of firms and factors to move freely and easily from one industry to another in search of the highest possible return.* Only in this way can supply and demand schedules move rightwards and leftwards, bringing about the needed adjustments of quantities and prices.

We have seen as well that this is by no means an easy set of conditions to achieve. With firms, as previously with factors, it rules out all legal barriers to interindustry movement, such as restrictive patents. But beyond this it implies that industries in which the initial scale of manufacture is very large cannot be considered as meeting the requirements for pure competition. In automobile or steel manufacturing, for example, in which the minimum size of plant entails an investment of millions of dollars, the degree of competitive pressure from "outside" entrepreneurs is obviously much less than in the stationery store business, where a newcomer can enter for an investment of a few thousand dollars.

Ease of exit is a no less necessary and equally demanding requirement. The competitive process will not shift about supply curves if some producers cannot withdraw their investments in land or capital and move them to alternative uses. Yet, as we have seen, this inability to move out can indeed retard adjustments of supply, particularly in industries with large fixed investments that are highly "specific" in their use. Such industries may go on producing even if they cannot cover their full costs, as long as their revenues bring in enough to nibble away at fixed expenses (see p. 94 n). Thus the problems of securing easy entry and exit further restricts the environment of pure competition to industries in which no large or technically specific investments are required.

3. *Nondifferentiated goods*

But even these strict conditions still do not define the state of competition we have implicitly assumed. It is possible for a market to consist of many small buyers and sellers, each operating with relatively simple equipment, and yet these firms may not compete fully against one another. This is the case when each firm sells a product that is *differenti-ated* (or distinguishable) from that of its competitors. For if there is a difference, however slight, between one man's product and another's, the demand curve for the product of each will be sloping rather than horizontal, even if the slope is very small. As a result, product differen-tiation will enable a seller to hold onto *some* of his trade even if his price is a trifle higher than his competitor's, whereas in a purely competitive market where goods and services are indistinguishable from one another, no marketer can depart in the slightest degree from the prevailing price.

There are markets in which perfectly anonymous undifferentiated commodities are sold—for example, the market for grain or for coal or for common labor, in which no seller can ask even a penny more for his product or services than the going price. In the great bulk of retail and wholesale markets, however, such totally undifferentiated products are the exception rather than the rule.

Why must commodities be exactly alike for a state of pure competi-tion to exist? The answer is that *only identical commodities compete solely on the basis of price.* Much of what we call "competition" in the impure markets of the real world consists in differentiating products through style, design, services, etc., so that they will *not* have to com-pete just on price. We shall look into this very common case of "imper-fect competition" in our next chapter. But we must rule it out as a permissible form of competition to bring about the exact results of our market analysis thus far. The essential rule for a purely competitive market is that the word "competition" must mean *price competition only.*

Competition in fact and theory

Obviously, pure competition is an extremely demanding state of affairs. It requires small and numerous firms selling identical products in a highly mobile and fluid environment. Does such a market in fact exist?

It has been customary to claim that farming constitutes a perfect example of pure competition, since its units are very numerous and its main products undifferentiated. But farming lacks one qualification. It has proved to be a very difficult occupation to move out of when prices fall. Of the roughly 3.7 million farms in the United States, about one million sell less than $5,000 worth of farm products a year and are, by any definition, uneconomical operations. Yet submarginal farmers are reluctant to leave an occupation that gives them at least a minimal security, for the frightening insecurity (and perhaps even worse eco-nomic luck) of the city.

The world of retailing qualifies much more readily in terms of easy entry and exit, and it is characterized by many small firms. But retailing loses out on the question of differentiation. The very essence of most retail establishments, even if they sell exactly the same wares as the competitor down the street (in fact, especially if they do), is to try to be "different."

Hence the search for perfect examples of pure competition is apt to end with very few cases. Why, then, do we spend so much time analyzing it?

The answer is twofold. In part it lies in the fact that as much as 40 or 50 per cent of the output of the nation comes from sectors that *resemble* — even though they do not exactly qualify for — pure competition. The service trades, the wholesale markets, much retailing, some raw material production are near enough to being "pure" in their competitive structures, so that we can apply the reasoning of price theory very closely in understanding the market results we see in those industries.

But there is a second reason as well. Even in those sectors or industries where pure competition obviously does not apply — in the monopolistic or oligopolistic situations with which our next chapter will be concerned — the mechanism of the market will still be clearly discernible. Supply and demand, factor productivities, marginal revenue and marginal cost will continue to be the prevailing guidelines. Hence we must understand the basic elements of microeconomics because most of them will still apply. And unless we know to what results these elements lead us in the ideal environment of pure competition, we will hardly be in a position to know what a difference monopoly or oligopoly make to the workings of the market system.

Summary

1. We divide costs within the firm into *fixed and variable costs.* Variable costs change with the addition or discharge of factors. Fixed costs are contractual costs or costs that are associated with the unchanged use of one factor. They do not vary with output.

2. Both fixed and variable (and total) costs are usually calculated *per unit of output. Fixed costs decline per unit of output as total output increases.*

3. *Variable costs first decline and then rise,* reflecting the increasing and then diminishing marginal productivity of the factors. The typical shape of the variable unit cost curve is *U-shaped* or *dish-shaped.*

4. Adding together fixed and variable costs, we get a *dish-shaped unit cost curve for the firm.*

5. The marginal cost curve shows us the actual operative factor at work. The relation of marginal and average figures to one another is such that the *marginal unit cost curve always cuts the average unit cost curve at the lowest point of the latter.*

6. *The competitive firm operates between two horizontal curves: The demand*

curve for its product is infinitely elastic. The supply curve of factors to itself is also infinitely elastic. That is, it can sell all it can profitably make without disturbing the market price, and it can hire or fire all the factors it wishes without disturbing their price. The only process under its control is the combination of factors to secure maximum efficiency.

7. *The point of maximum profit is that output where marginal revenue just equals marginal cost.* In a competitive market for a single firm, marginal revenue and average revenue are both equal to price. Therefore it pushes its output until the marginal cost of the last unit just equals price. Any output more than this would incur losses, and any output less than this would fail to gain all potential profit.

8. If a competitive firm enjoys profits in this position of *MC = MR,* it will experience *an influx of firms from other areas.* This will cause industry supply to increase and prices to fall. Conversely, if it experiences a loss, there will be a gradual *exodus of firms* until supply for the industry falls and prices rise.

9. The *equilibrium point for the competitive firm is reached when marginal revenue equals marginal cost, and average cost equals price.* At this point there is no incentive for the entrepreneur to alter his scale of output or for firms to leave or enter the industry.

10. In a competitive market, the *marginal* firm enjoys no profit. Intramarginal firms may have quasi rents.

11. In addition to changes in cost from moving along a fixed unit cost curve, firms can enjoy *economies of scale,* provided that the technology of the industry leads to these. At some point, economies of scale cease and the long-run cost curve again turns up.

12. In addition, *external economies or diseconomies* can affect the cost curves of all firms within an industry. For most industries a condition of roughly *constant* long-term costs seems to prevail.

13. The environment of the firm is assumed at first to be that of pure competition. By this we mean a market in which there are:

    • *Large numbers of marketers.* As a result, each faces a market situation, both with regard to factors and goods, in which his own actions are powerless to affect prices. Only the factor mix is under the control of the competitive entrepreneur.
    • *Ease of exit and entry.* This requires the absence of all barriers to mobility, including that of size and technical specificity.
    • *Nondifferentiated products.* This insures the restriction of competition to price alone.

14. Pure competition is obviously rarely found in actuality. But it does describe the actions of some markets tolerably well and it provides a bench mark from which to measure the degree of competition that we find in the real world.

Questions

1. If you were a retail grocer, what kinds of costs would be fixed for you? Variable? If you were a manufacturer who owned a large computer, would its maintenance be a fixed cost? If you *rented* the computer, would it be?

2. Assume that your fixed costs are $500 a week and that your output can vary

from 100 to 1,000 units, given the scale of your enterprise. Graph what happens to fixed costs per unit.

3. Assume that your plant hires 10 men successively, and that output changes as follows:

Number of men	Total output per week
1	100 units
2	300
3	550
4	700
5	750
6	800

What is the marginal productivity of each man? If each worker costs you $100 per week, what is the variable cost per unit as you add men?

4. If you now add fixed costs of $500 per week to the variable cost you have just ascertained, what is the average cost per unit? What is the marginal cost per unit? (Remember, this is figured by dividing the *change in total cost* by the *change in total output*).

5. Graph the curve of average total unit costs and marginal unit costs. Why does the marginal unit cost curve cross the average unit cost curve at its lowest point?

6. What does average revenue mean and what is its relation to price? What is meant by marginal revenue? Why is marginal revenue the same as average revenue for a competitive firm?

7. Explain carefully why a competitive firm operates between two horizontal curves, one on the demand side and one on the factor supply side.

8. Suppose that the price per unit at which you sell the output of your firm (in the example above) is $1.35. Draw in such a marginal revenue curve. Now very carefully indicate where the MR and MC curves meet. Show on the diagram the output corresponding to this point. What is the approximate average cost at this output? Is there a profit here? Indicate by letters the rectangle that shows the profit per unit of output and the number of units.

9. What will be the result, in a competitive industry, of such a profit? Draw a diagram showing how an influx of firms can change the ruling market price. Will it be higher or lower?

10. Draw a diagram showing how price could drop below the lowest point on the average total unit cost curve, and indicate the loss the firm would suffer.

11. Carefully draw a diagram showing the equilibrium position for the firm. What is the relation of MC, MR, and P at this point? If MC = MR, does this mean that the entrepreneur is now motivated to alter his output? If AC = P, what does this mean as to the movement of firms into or out of the industry?

12. Suppose that you are a druggist, and you know that the least efficient druggist in town makes virtually no profit at all. Assuming that you sell in the same market as he does at the same prices and that you hire factors at the same prices also, what causes could bring about a profit to your enterprise? What would you expect to be the trend of these profits?

13. Would you expect economies of scale from greatly enlarging your drugstore? Why or why not?

14. Do you think as the entire drugstore business expands it enjoys external economies or suffers from external diseconomies? How about the gold-mining business?

15. Is the drugstore business an example of pure competition? Explain carefully in what ways it might qualify and in what ways it might not.

7

Competition in the real world

Monopoly (and nowadays oligopoly) are bad words to most people, just as competition is a good word. But with the one as with the other, not everyone can specify exactly what is bad about them. Often we get the impression that the aims of the monopolist are evil and grasping, while those of the competitor are wholesome and altruistic, and therefore the essential difference between a world of pure competition and one of very impure competition is one of motives and drives — of well-meaning competitors and ill-intentioned monopolists.

The truth is that *exactly the same motives drive the monopoly and the competitive firm*. Both seek to maximize their profits. Indeed, the competitive firm, placed in a situation in which it must keep careful track of costs and revenues in order to survive is apt to be, if anything, *more* penny-pinching and more intensely profit-oriented than the monopolist who (as we shall see) can afford to take a less hungry attitude toward profits. The lesson to be learned — and it is an important one — is that motives have nothing to do with the problem of less-than-pure competition. *The difference between a monopoly, an oligopoly, and a situation of pure competition is entirely one of market structure* — that is, of the number of firms, ease of entry or exit, and the degree of differentiation among their goods.

Price-takers and price-searchers

We have already noted a very precise distinction between the competitive situation, with its numerous firms and undifferentiated goods, and markets in which the number of sellers is few or in which goods are highly differentiated. In the competitive case, as we have seen, each firm caters to so small a section of the market that the demand curve for its produce is, for all intents and purposes, horizontal. By way of contrast, in a monopolistic or oligopolistic market structure there are so few firms that each one faces a distinctly sloping demand curve. That means that each firm, by varying its output, can affect the price for its product.

Another way of describing this difference is to call purely competitive firms, who have no control over their price, *price-takers* and to label monopolies or oligopolies or any firm that can affect the price of its product, *price-searchers.*

"Pure" monopolies

By examining the economic problems faced by a "pure" monopoly, let us see how such a price-searcher operates. Why do we place the word "pure" in quotes? Because a monopoly is not as easy to define as one might think. Essentially, the word means that there is only *one* seller of a particular good or service. The trouble comes in defining the "particular" good or service. In a sense, any seller of a differentiated good is a monopolist, for no one else dispenses *quite* the same utilities as he does: each shoeshine boy has his "own" customers, some of whom would probably continue to patronize his stand even if he charged slightly more than his competition.

Thus at one end of the difficulty is the fact that there is an element of monopoly in many seemingly competitive goods—a complication we shall come back to later. At the other end of the problem is that even where there is only one seller of a commodity—say the telephone company—there are still *substitutes* for its service. We can send a telegram or write a letter if telephoning becomes too expensive. Thus, before we can draw conclusions from the mere fact that a company provides the "only" service of a kind, we need to know how easy or difficult it is to switch into other products or services.

The limits of monopoly

Evidently the problem of defining a "pure" monopoly is not easily resolved. Let us, however, assume that we will all agree to call the local power company a monopoly, because no one else sells gas and electricity to the community. In Fig. 7-1 we show what the demand curve of such a monopoly looks like.

One point is immediately clear. *The monopolistic firm faces the same kind of demand curve that the competitive industry faces.* That is because it caters to *all* the demand for that particular product, just as does

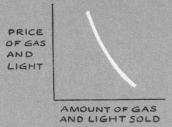

PRICE
OF GAS
AND
LIGHT

DEMAND CURVE
FOR A
MONOPOLY

AMOUNT OF GAS
AND LIGHT SOLD

FIG. 7-1

the industrial group of competitive firms. A corollary follows. The monopolist faces a fundamental limitation on his power to control the market imposed by the demand curve itself. Suppose a monopolist is selling quantity *OX* at price *OA* as shown in Fig. 7-2. He would like to sell quantity *OY* at price *OA*, but *he cannot*. He has no way of forcing the market to take a larger quantity of his product—unless he lowers the price to *OB*.*

The situation is very similar (on the seller's side) with a *union*. A union can raise the price of labor, since it controls the supply of labor, but it cannot force employers to hire more labor than they want. Hence the question "Can unions raise wages?" must be answered "Yes," insofar as those who continued to be hired are concerned. But until we know the elasticity of the demand for labor, we cannot say if unions can raise the total amount of labor's revenues. (Recall our analysis on p. 80.)

There is one thing a monopolist can do, however, that neither a union nor a purely competitive firm can. He can advertise and thus seek to move the demand curve for his product to the right. Advertising does not "pay" for a purely competitive firm selling undifferentiated goods,

---

*What would be the *most* profitable course for the monopolist to follow? It would be to sell his goods at *varying* prices, charging more when the buyer is willing and able to pay a high price. (One could imagine an auction, for example, in which a monopolist doled out his product in this manner.) We call this *discriminatory pricing*. Why does the monopolist not follow it? (1) In some industries it is illegal. (2) It is extremely difficult to carry out, because someone with a low personal demand could pay more than he himself wanted of a good, in order to resell it to someone higher up on the demand curve. If this trading among customers goes on, the final average price will be exactly that established by the demand curve and the supply schedule. Nevertheless, discriminatory pricing is not uncommon in certain fields: antiques, used cars, pawnshops—and perhaps some professional fees.

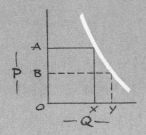

DEMAND CURVE
AS A CONSTRAINT
ON THE
MONOPOLIST

FIG. 7-2

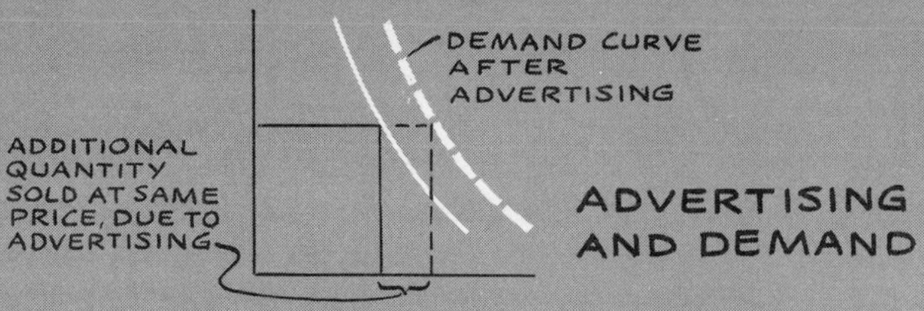

FIG. 7-3

ADDITIONAL QUANTITY SOLD AT SAME PRICE, DUE TO ADVERTISING

DEMAND CURVE AFTER ADVERTISING

ADVERTISING AND DEMAND

for such a firm has no way of being sure that *its* goods—and not a competitor's—will benefit: imagine a single farmer advertising "Buy wheat!" But advertising *can* pay for a monopolist who will get all the demand he can conjure up. We can think of advertising as an attempt to sell larger quantities of a good or service without reducing prices, by shifting the demand curve itself. Figure 7-3 shows us this important effect.

Cost curves for the monopolist

We have seen in what way the shape of the demand curves faced by monopolists differs from those faced by competitive firms. Are costs curves similarly different?

In general, they are not. We can take the cost profile of a monopoly as being exactly the same as that of a competitive firm. The monopoly, like the competitive firm, buys factors and exerts no control over their prices. A.T.& T. does not affect the level of wages or the price of land or capital by its decisions to expand production or not.* The monopolist, like the competitive entrepreneur, experiences the effects of changing productivity as he hires additional factors, and again like the competitive firm, he shops for the best buy in the factor markets. Thus the same U-shaped average cost curve and the same more steeply sloped marginal cost curve will describe the cost changes experienced by a monopolist quite as well as those of a competitive firm.

Monopoly revenues

It is when we come to the revenue side of the picture that we meet the critical distinction of monopoly. Unlike a competitive firm, *a monopoly has a marginal revenue curve that is different from its average revenue*

*There is a special situation in which there is only one *buyer*, that we call "monopsony." A large employer who is the only substantial buyer of labor in a small town may be a monopsonist, and his decisions to hire labor or land or capital *will* affect their prices. For the monopsonist, the marginal cost curve is affected not only by the changing productivity of a factor but by its varying price, as more and more of the factor is hired. Because this is a situation infrequently found in the marketplace, we shall not analyze it further here. The principles involved are in no way different from those of monopoly.

curve. The difference arises because each time a monopolist sells more output, he must reduce his price, whereas a competitive firm sells its larger output at the same price. Therefore, the revenue yielded to the monopolist by each additional unit will not be as great as that of the preceding unit whose price was higher.

A table may make this clear. Let us suppose we have a monopoly that is faced with an average revenue or price schedule as in Table 7-1.

**TABLE
7 • 1**

Price	Quantity sold	Total revenue	Marginal revenue	Marg. rev. per unit (change in rev. ÷ change in units)
20	1,000	$20,000	$20,000	$20
19	2,000	38,000	18,000	18
18	3,000	54,000	16,000	16
17	4,000	68,000	14,000	14
16	5,000	80,000	12,000	12
15	6,000	90,000	10,000	10

The graph of such a marginal revenue curve looks like Fig. 7-4.

What determines the shape of the marginal revenue curve? Obviously, the change in demand that will be brought about by a drop in price. In turn, this reflects the elasticity of demand which, in turn, hinges on our tastes, the availability of substitutes, and so on.

Equilibrium for the monopoly

The next step is obvious enough. We must superimpose the cost profile and the revenue profile to determine the equilibrium position for the monopolist. We can see it in Fig. 7-5.

What will be the equilibrium position? *The monopolist who seeks to maximize profit is guided by exactly the same rule as the competitive firm: he adds factors so long as the marginal revenue they bring in is*

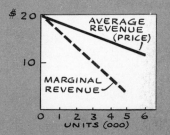

AVERAGE AND
MARGINAL REVENUE
FOR A
MONOPOLIST

FIG. 7-4

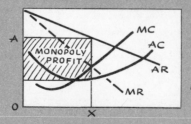

FIG. 7-5

EQUILIBRIUM
FOR THE
MONOPOLIST

greater than their marginal cost. Hence we look for the intersection of the *MC* and *MR* curves on Fig. 7-5. Now if we extend a vertical line down to the horizontal axis, we will discover how much output will be produced (*OX*) at what price (*OA*). (See Fig. 7-7.)

And what will the profit be? As before, profit is the difference between *average* cost and *average* revenue. The intersection of the *MC* and *MR* curves determines in the first place what our output will be; and now knowing that, we can tell what our average cost and price, or average revenue, will be. Hence we can easily block in the profit of the enterprise. We do this in Fig. 7-6.

Monopoly vs. competitive prices

What is the difference between this price and that of a purely competitive market? We remember the formula for the equilibrium price of such a market: Price = *MC* = *MR* = *AC*. In the monopoly situation *MC* still equals *MR* (this is always the profit-maximizing guide), but price certainly does not equal *AC*. Whereas the competitive firm is forced to price its goods at the lowest point on its cost curve, the monopolist sells at a price far above cost. Then, too, there is no pressure from "outside" forcing the monopolist to reduce costs. Hence his entire cost curve may well lie above that of a competitive industry producing the same product. It is interesting to note that when hard pressed, some big auto firms (not even monopolies) have reduced overhead expenses by as much as a third. But most of the time, monopolies are not hard pressed.

If this were the case in a competitive market, we know what the remedy would be. An influx of firms would move the supply curve to the right; and as a result, prices would fall until excess profits had been wiped out. But in a monopoly situation, by the very definition of a monopoly, there is no entry into the market. Hence the monopolist is

MONOPOLY
PROFIT

FIG. 7-6

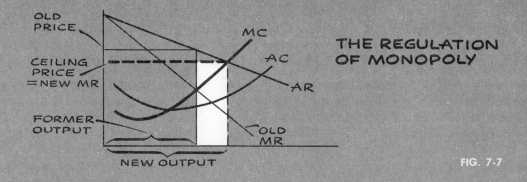

FIG. 7-7

able to restrict his output to the amount that will bring in the high price he enjoys.

Monopoly thus imposes two burdens on society. It sells wares at a *higher price* than that of the competitive firm, and its *output is smaller* than would be the case under competitive conditions. The consumer gets less and pays more for it.

This is not, as we have had occasion to remark before, a full accounting of the "social cost" of monopoly. It is a description of the *economic* difference between the market solution of a competitive and a monopolistic firm. It ignores entirely such matters as power or influence, which may make monopoly politically undesirable, and it omits as well any consideration of the possible usefulness of some monopolies (like the phone company) in providing a unified service or considerable economies of large-scale production.

Finally, we should note that most "natural" monopolies, such as the utility companies or water supply companies or the telephone company, are regulated by public authorities. By imposing price ceilings on these monopolies (usually calculated to allow the companies to earn a "fair return" on their invested capital), the regulating commissions seek to approximate the results of a competitive environment. As Fig. 7-7 shows, its MR will be horizontal along the price ceiling, just like that of a competitive firm, and therefore its output will expand.

Oligopoly

Monopoly in its "pure" form is a rarity, and unregulated monopoly is rarer still.* From our acquaintance with the American economy, we

---

*How do we recognize a monopoly? Because of the problem of substitutes, there is no very clear sign, except in a few cases such as the "natural" monopolies discussed above. Usually when we speak of "monopolies" we mean (a) very large businesses, (b) with much higher than competitive profits, and (c) with relatively little direct product competition. Not many firms satisfy all three conditions. GM or Standard Oil is a monopoly by criteria *a* and *b*, but not by *c;* Polaroid by *b* and *c* but not *a*. Note, furthermore, that even small businesses can be monopolies, such as "the only gambling house in town" famed in all Westerns.

113

know that the market structure in which most big corporations operate is not that of pure monopoly, but rather that of oligopoly. In an oligopolistic market situation, a *few* sellers divide the market and typically compete with one another by means of advertising, product differentiation, service, etc., rather than by the classic competitive means of price.

What does a typical oligopoly look like under the lens of price theory? On the cost side, it is much the same as a monopolist or a perfect competitor. There is, however, an essential difference between the demand curve of a monopolist and that of an oligopolist. The demand curve for a monopolist, since it comprises the entire demand for the commodity, is the downward sloping curve of the kind with which we are familiar. But the demand curve for an oligopolist, although it is also downward sloping, has a shape that is new to us and quite unusual.

Suppose that you were the president of a large company that, along with three other very similar companies, sold roughly 80 per cent of a certain commodity. Suppose also that a price had been established for your commodity. It yielded you and your competitors a "reasonable" profit, but you and your fellow officers were considering how that profit might be increased.

One possibility that would certainly be discussed would be to raise the price of your product and hope that your customers would continue to be loyal to you. But your company economists might point out that their analyses showed a very elastic demand for your product *if you raised your price, but your competitors did not*. That is, at the higher price, many of your "loyal" customers would switch to a competitive brand, so that your revenues would fall sharply and your profits decline.

Suppose, then, you took the other tack and gambled on that very elasticity of demand by cutting your prices. Would not other firms' customers switch to you and thereby raise your revenues and profits? This time your advisors might point out that if you cut your price, your competitors would almost certainly do the same, to prevent you from taking a portion of "their" market. As a result, with prices cut all around, you would probably find demand highly *inelastic,* and your revenues not larger but smaller.

As Fig. 7-8 shows, you are facing a *kinked* demand curve. In the situation, you might well be tempted to sit tight and do nothing.

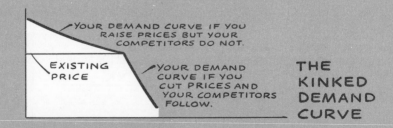

FIG. 7-8

The kinked demand curve helps explain why oligopoly prices are often so unvarying even without collusion among firms, but it does not really explain how the existing price is arrived at. For once cost or demand conditions have changed enough to overcome oligopolistic inertia, a new "kink" will again appear around the changed price. The kinked curve thus shows what forces affect *changes* in the oligopolistic situation, rather than how supply and demand originally determine the going price.

Price theory, as such, does not shed as much light on how the price of steel or cars or tires or tin cans is arrived at, as it does in a fully competitive industry. But why should this be so? We know in general what the demand curves look like for oligopolistic commodities, and we have a general idea of their supply behavior. Does it not follow therefore that price will be set by the standard supply-and-demand interplay?

The maximizing assumption

The answer — or rather, the lack of a clear-cut answer — causes us to examine another underpinning of classical price theory. We have already looked into the assumptions of pure competition — indeed, in this chapter we are tracing the consequences of failing to meet those assumptions. But the oligopoly problem forces us to confront a second fundamental premise of microeconomic theory. This is the assumption that firms maximize short-run profits.

Under pure competition, as we have seen, such profit maximization has a powerful motive working for it, quite above that of an entrepreneur's desire to get rich. This is the motive of *self-preservation*. Firms that do not constantly equate marginal cost and marginal revenue — the iron rule of maximizing — will simply fail to survive the competitive test. Hence, in the classical model, we can accept short-run profit maximizing as a fair description of reality, as well as a valid guideline for a well-working market system.

Not so, however, with oligopoly or monopoly. To be sure, a great corporation that failed to make any profits for many years would eventually fail, but there is little danger that a large company will go under if it does not make the last dollar — or even the last ten million dollars — of possible profits in any one year or even over two or three years running.

Oligopolistic indeterminacy

Do the great oligopolistic concerns try to equate marginal cost and marginal revenue, and thus maximize their income?

This is a question that is difficult to answer, by virtue of the very indeterminacy of the oligopolistic equilibrium resting point. We have just seen that a kinked demand curve makes likely a very high degree of oligopolistic inertia. The classic route to higher profits—beating one's competitor on price—tends to be shunned. What we find instead of the single-minded pursuit of gain is a strategic pursuit of long-run growth and strength that may very well lead to short-run decisions *not* to make as much money as possible.

Two factors in particular make the oligopolist's day-by-day behavior difficult to predict in theory. The first is his limited but not insignificant ability to influence the demand curve for his own product. Oligopolies are typically the largest advertisers, for one way in which competition *can* be carried out without disturbing the price structure is by inducing customers to switch brands at the same price.* Thus a considerable degree of oligopolistic success depends not on pursuing the traditional course of profit-maximizing, but on pursuing a successful strategy of sale-enlargement.

Second, the *long-term* considerations that guide the behavior of oligopolies introduce a new element into the profit-maximizing picture that is missing in the competitive case. The entrepreneur of the small firm lives in a world in which his costs and his demand curve are both subject to change without notice. He must do the best he can, at each moment, to obtain the highest income for himself. The oligopolist, on the other hand, has considerable degree of control over his future. Since his overhead costs are usually high, he is able to make stringent economies if the need arises. And since he lives in a market situation where he is reasonably sure of not having to face price competition, he plans for the future in terms of improving or changing his product or his advertising or both.

This necessarily introduces into his plans a *time dimension* of much greater depth than in the case of classic competition. And in turn, the ability—not to say necessity—to plan several years in advance gives greater latitude to whatever decisions may be in the best immediate interests of the firm. *Thus profit-maximizing, however valid as a description of the state of mind or aim of the oligopolist, no longer serves, as it does in the competitive case, to describe the exact price and output decisions that we can expect firms to undertake in the face of market pressures.* Oligopolies are, within broad limits, free to follow whatever course—aggressive or defensive—their managements decide is best, and competing oligopolies have often followed *different* courses. Hence

---

*Thus we find a new kind of cost in oligopolistic firms—*selling* cost, or cost incurred, not to hire factors of production and thereby directly to increase output, but to move the demand curve and thereby to increase sales. A competitive firm has no selling costs, because its product is indistinguishable from that of anyone else.

microtheory can say relatively little about how the market will impinge on the oligopolistic firm, since its economic pressures are much less imperious than they are in pure competition.

From oligopoly to imperfect competition

We shall return once more to an assessment of the market under the conditions of oligopoly, but we must first finish our review of the marketplace in reality, rather than theory. For oligopoly, although perhaps the most striking departure from the ideal of pure competition, is not the most common departure. Once we pass from the manufacturing to the retail or service sectors where competition is still intense and "atomistic" (i.e., characterized by numerous small units), we encounter a new kind of market situation, equally strange to the pages of a text on pure competition. This is a situation in which there are many firms, with relatively easy entrance and exit, but in which *each firm sells a product slightly differentiated from that of every other.* Here is the world of the average store or the small competitive manufacturer of a brand-name product — indeed, of every seller who can "identify" his product to the public and who must face the competition of many other makers of similar but not exactly identical products.

Economists call this market situation in which there is a tinge of monopoly *imperfect competition* or *monopolistic competition.* How does it differ from pure competition? Once again, there is no difference on the cost side, which is exactly the same for both a perfectly competitive and an imperfectly competitive firm. The difference, again, comes in the nature of the demand curve.

We recall that the special attribute of the demand curve facing a firm in a purely competitive situation is its horizontal character. By way of contrast, *in a market of imperfect competition, the demand curve facing each seller slopes gently downward.* As we have already seen, this is because his good or service is not exactly like that of his competitors, and because he therefore has some ability to raise price without losing all his business.

Equilibrium in monopolistic competition

What is the equilibrium position of such an imperfectly competitive firm — say a dress manufacturer? In Fig. 7-9, we show, on the left, an imperfect competitor who is obviously making substantial profits. Note that his best position where $MR = MC$ is *exactly* like that of a monopolist.

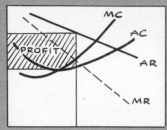

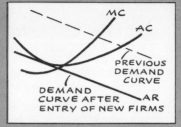

BEFORE OTHER FIRMS ENTER   AFTER OTHER FIRMS ENTER

FIG. 7-9

But our firm is not a monopolist, and its profits are therefore not immune to erasure by entry into its field. In Fig. 7-9, we show the same firm after *other entrepreneurs have moved into the industry* (with additional similar, although not identical, products) and thereby taken away some of our firm's market and moved its demand curve to the left.

Note that our final position for the marginal dress firm has no more profit than that of a purely competitive seller. On the other hand, because his demand curve slopes, the equilibrium point cannot be at the lowest point on the average cost curve, nor will output have reached optimum size. (Of course, intramarginal firms can be more profitable than the marginal case we have graphed.)

This outcome clearly dissipates economic well-being. The fact that firms are forced to operate to the left of the optimums on their cost curves means that *they have not been able to combine factors to yield their greatest efficiency*—a failure that penalizes factors, once when they are paid too little because their potential marginal productivity has not been reached, and again as consumers when they are forced to pay too much for products that have not been produced at lowest possible cost. In addition, wastage is incurred because the attempt to differentiate products leads in many instances to too many small units—for example, the famous (and all too common) case of four gas stations on one corner.

Inefficient though it may be, just as in a purely competitive industry, monopolistic competition yields the marginal firm in an industry no profit. The entrepreneur therefore feels fully as hard-pressed as would the producer of an undifferentiated commodity. The difference is that a monopolistic competitive businessman has the possibility of *further differentiating* his product, hoping thereby to tilt his demand curve in a more inelastic position. In turn, this might allow him to raise his prices slightly and to squeeze out a tiny "pure monopoly" profit. The result is that we find a tremendous variety of goods in industries in which monopolistic competition is typical—the ladies garment industry being a prime example.*

---

*Oligopolists as well as monopolistic competitors march to the drums of competition through product differentiation. In the fields of cigarettes, soaps, and breakfast cereals, the market is pretty much made up of three firms, and thirty or forty years ago most grocery

The extent of market imperfection

How much of the whole market system is imperfect in one sense or another?

Let us begin with pure monopolies. We have seen how difficult it is to define what such a monopoly is; but if we are not too careful about looking for product substitutes, then perhaps we can classify 10 to 20 per cent of output as monopolistic. Nearly all of it is the output of public utilities, regulated by public agencies, or consists of the output of the public sector (for the government is certainly a monopoly, although not a profit-maximizing one).

Oligopolies constitute a more significant category. Roughly speaking, we can say that most *industrial* output takes place in markets with at least some degree of oligopolistic structure. In manufacturing generally, 97 giant corporations out of 124,200 in 1954 owned 42 per cent of all assets in the field. As another general measure, the top 500 industrial companies—a tenth of 1 per cent of all industrial corporations—do one-third of all industrial business. Such statistics make it clear that giant business occupies a place in the economy out of all proportion to its minuscule numerical strength.

Over-all statistics, however, do not tell us much about the structure of individual markets. From market to market the degree of oligopolization varies widely, reaching a high point in autos, tin cans, and cigarettes, where the top four companies do up to 90 per cent of all the business in the field, down through medium-concentrated industries such as steel (where the top four do about half the nation's business), to the least concentrated—and yet by no means purely competitive—industries, such as bottled soft drinks, where the leading four companies sell only 10 per cent of all output.

The last statistic alerts us further, however, to the difficulty of describing the market itself. If by "bottled soft drinks" we mean colas, then clearly that particular market is highly oligopolized with Pepsi-Cola and Coca-Cola as leaders in the trade. But if we mean by "bottled drinks" a larger range of substitutes including orange pop, ginger ales, etc., then the degree of oligopolization thins out markedly. Similarly, the problem of measuring or even defining oligopoly is complicated by the geographic definition of the market. For example, the top eight beer and ale companies sell only 28 per cent of the nation's total consumption of beer; but because these drinks are usually produced and marketed within a limited region, the concentration among brewers is much greater

---

stores stocked only about three or four brands of each. But today the shelves holding these products have been expanded again and again as each of the three firms came forward with a new differentiation or one to match a new, highly successful one of its competitor.

in any one area, such as New York or Chicago or Los Angeles, than it is in the nation as a whole.

Can we extract from this highly complicated panorama a general indication of the extent of oligopolization? Perhaps the best we can do is to hazard the following generalizations: (1) about 30 to 40 per cent of final output can be classified as within an oligopolistic market—that is, a market in which the number of significant sellers is too few to be called, by any stretch of the term, "competitive"; (2) the degree of oligopolization in these markets shows wide variation—in roughly half of them the top eight companies do at least one-third of the business in that market; (3) the extent of oligopolization within markets and the number of oligopolized markets do not seem to be increasing.*

It is much more difficult, perhaps even impossible, to measure the exact extent of monopolistic competition. As we have already discussed, very few industries fully meet the qualifications of pure competition; and even if we remove the proviso of easy entry and exit, not much of America's output is both undifferentiated in character and produced by many firms. Only agriculture, fisheries, and a few other industries comprising no more than 10 or 15 per cent of the nation's final output could then be called purely competitive. If we added another 30 to 40 per cent of output as coming from recognizably oligopolistic market structures, plus 10 to 20 per cent of "pure" monopoly, this leaves us something between a low of 35 per cent and a high of 50 per cent of output in market structures that would be called monopolistically competitive.

These estimates are not to be taken as more than very rough orders of magnitude—educated guesses. Nonetheless, with all their margin of uncertainty, they unmistakeably show one thing. Market imperfection in one form or another is the reality that mainly describes the macro system we find in the United States (or any other industrial nation). What significance does this have for the effectiveness of the market system, or for the relevance of the theory that seeks to describe that system? These are the culminating questions to which our last chapter will seek to provide some answers.

---

*Why is the trend toward further oligopolization static? The answer is a complex one. In part we can trace the reasons to the impact of antitrust legislation that has prevented or impeded many oligopoly-producing mergers. In part it is due to the expansion of large firms into unrelated fields (diversification), which tends to spread, rather than concentrate, their economic power. Partly also it may be traceable to the increased bureaucratization of corporate management.

Summary

1. The motives of monopoly and oligopoly are exactly those of competition. What is different is the *structure of the market* in which these motives give rise to action.

2. The monopoly or oligopoly faces a sloping rather than a horizontal demand curve. It is a *price-searcher rather than a price-taker*.

3. A monopoly is difficult to define narrowly because of the existence of *substitutes* for all commodities. The monopolistic *firm* enjoys the same demand curve as does the competitive *industry*, and is forced to obey the limitations imposed by its demand curve. It can, however, attempt to *shift the curve to the right by advertising*.

4. The cost curves of monopolists and oligopolists are shaped the same as those of competitive firms. However, monopolists face *marginal revenue curves that are not identical with their average revenue curves*. The difference arises because the monopolist must lower his price to increase his sales. Therefore, each additional unit brings in a smaller addition to total revenues than the previous unit brought.

5. Equilibrium for the monopoly (as for the competitive firm) is that output where $MR = MC$. This is the point of maximum profit. AC will not equal P, however, for there is no influx of firms to push prices down to this point.

6. The result of monopoly is twofold: prices will be higher than in competitive firms, and output will be smaller.

7. Oligopoly is a more common market structure than monopoly. It is characterized by a few sellers, rather than one.

8. The oligopolist's *demand curve is typically kinked*. This shape reflects the difficulty of holding his market share if he raises prices alone, and the difficulty of maintaining his price advantage if he cuts price, which will be quickly followed by his fellow oligopolists.

9. Oligopolies often need not obey the dictates of *short-run* profit maximizing. On the contrary, they can plan considerable distances into the future. As a result, *profit-maximizing*, however accurate a description of their goal, *does not lead to the exactly predictable behavior* that it does in the case of the competitive firm.

10. Imperfect or monopolistic competition is used to describe markets in which there are *many sellers selling differentiated products*. The point of difference is the existence of a *slightly sloping demand curve*.

11. Imperfect competition leads to two main results. First, output *does not reach the point of lowest cost* and greatest efficiency, thereby penalizing both consumers and factors. Second, there is a tendency for *differentiation to increase* in the hope of gaining a small profit.

12. The bulk of all markets in industrial countries are *imperfect to some degree*. Pure competition is perhaps as rare as "pure" monopoly.

Questions

1. In what way, if any, do the motives of a monopolist differ from those of a perfect competitor? In what way does the time span of his decision-making differ? Can this affect his behavior (as contrasted to his motivation)?

2. How would you define a monopoly? Are monopolies necessarily large? What constraints does a demand curve put on the behavior of a monopoly?

3. Suppose that you were the only seller of a certain kind of machinery in the nation. Suppose further that you discovered that your demand curve looked like this:

Price	Quantity of machines sold
$100	5,000
90	6,000
80	7,500
70	10,000

   What is the average revenue at each price? What is the marginal revenue at each price? (Remember, you calculate marginal revenue by taking the *change* in receipts and dividing by the *change* in units.) Draw a diagram showing the marginal and average revenue.

4. Now superimpose on this diagram a hypothetical cost profile for your business. Where is the point of equilibrium for the monopolist? Is this the same, in terms of *MC* and *MR*, as the point for the competitive firm? Now show the equilibrium output and price.

5. Does the equilibrium output of the monopolist yield a profit? What are the relevant costs for figuring profit, average costs per unit, or marginal costs? Show on your diagram the difference between average cost and selling price.

6. Why will a monopolist's selling price not be pushed to the lowest point on the cost curve?

7. What is the difference between monopoly and oligopoly? Between oligopoly and pure competition? Between pure competition and monopolistic (or imperfect) competition? Between the latter and oligopoly?

8. What is meant by the kinked demand curve of an oligopolist? How do you explain the kink?

9. Why does the profit-maximizing assumption lead to such clear-cut results when we speak of pure competition, and to such indeterminate ones for oligopolies? Does the answer have something to do with the time over which the consequences of actions can be calculated?

10. What is a differentiated commodity? Give examples. Draw the demand curve for a farmer selling wheat and that for a toy manufacturer selling his own brand of dolls. What will happen if the doll manufacturer makes a large profit? What will his final point of equilibrium look like if he has many competitors?

11. Compare on two diagrams the equilibrium of the purely competitive firm and of the imperfectly competitive one. Show, by a dotted line, what the demand curve would look like for the imperfectly competitive firm if its product differentiation were removed. Where would its output now be located? What would be its selling price? Would the consumer gain from this?

8

The market system
in review

It is time to sit back and review our findings on the market system as a whole. In particular, we want to inquire what light the study of microeconomics throws on the working of the market system in real life.

Let us begin by recalling briefly the nature of the task we undertook. We began our excursion into microeconomics by asking what kind of order could be discerned in the apparent confusion of the marketplace. Did the throng of marketers exert some form of control over the goods and services produced by the firms that sought their business? What principles underlay the various levels of pay which those firms handed over to the marketers when they hired them? What kind of discipline was exerted by the market over the crucial production processes carried on by the firms themselves?

To all these questions, microtheory gave us clear answers within the assumptions of short-run profit maximizing and intense price competition characteristic of the world of atomistic firms it portrayed. Rather than review these answers in specific detail, let us try to summarize the meaning of the market's performance from an over-all point of view.

Two attributes of the system immediately call themselves to our attention:

1. *The fragmentation of economic power*

In the world of pure competition, only three forces ultimately direct the workings of the marketplace. One of these is, of course, the willingness and ability of the public to buy the goods and services offered to them. A second is the willingness and ability of the public, as a work force, to offer its services for production. The third is

123

the technological capability of the firm. In this way, *product demand, factor supply, and marginal productivity emerge as the basic controllers of the economic system*—or to put it differently, the psychological desires and dislikes of the public, on the one hand, and the realities of nature and man's ability to control it, on the other.

To be sure, the system requires for its operation another active force—the profit-seeking firm. Note, however, that the firm is singularly devoid of any capacity to influence the background elements we have mentioned. Driven by competition in an environment without shelter, the firm must obey the dictates of the public, both as buyers of goods and as suppliers of factor services, and can in no way impose its own dictates upon the public. Only in the choice of methods of production does it have a free hand, and here, if it does not measure up to average levels of performance, it will not long survive.

Hence, in a world of pure competition, and only such a world, the public becomes the repository of most economic power. This is often called the "sovereignty of the consumer," but it goes beyond that to the joint sovereignty of the consumer and the worker (or factor of production). In this way a society of pure competition comes closer than any other form of economic organization to translating the general ideas of political democracy into economic reality.

2. *The maximization of efficiency*

In a world of pure competition, as we have seen, output is pushed along each firm's supply curve until the lowest average unit cost is reached. There the firm must maintain its operation. This equation of marginal cost and revenue, and of price and average cost, is not merely a textbook solution to the problem of equilibrium. Rather, it represents a social solution to the problem of production that gives us the *largest possible volume of output, at the lowest possible prices compatible with existing resources, technology, and the consumption demands of the public.*

As we know, this is achieved because the firm must combine its factors of production with one eye on their relative cost and the other on their relative productivities, finally bringing about a mix in which each factor is used as effectively as possible, given its cost. At the same time, each factor is not only assigned to the post that utilizes it most efficiently, but competition in the factor market assures that each factor will be remunerated in full for its contribution to the firm's output. Any firm that fails to pay its factors in accord with their marginal productivities or combines them in a way that lessens their effectiveness will pay the price of seeing its factors bid away to other producers or of simply being undersold on the market. Thus, under the pressure of the system, *the full potential of all human and material resources will be used up to the limits imposed by the willingness and ability of individuals to work.*

The imperfect market

All these miraculous results of the market describe a system of pure competition. Yet, if there is any certainty in the world in which we live, it is that such a system is an unattainable goal. Merely consider what would have to be done to achieve a market structure in which pure competition would appear. Every giant firm (and many medium-sized ones) would have to be broken into fragments, none large enough to account for a significant fraction of the markets it served. Brand names familiar to every householder and worth millions of dollars to their owners would have to be outlawed, and the faceless output of undifferentiated commodities would have to take their place. All barriers to entry and to factor mobility would have to go: unions, patent restrictions, tariffs, initiation fees, inheritances. Even if it were unambiguously clear that the resulting system would be preferable to our own, it is obvious that such an assault on the present market system would never be tolerated—by the public any more than by the business sector.

And then, would it be unambiguously superior? We have deferred until now a full judgment on the effect of monopolistic imperfections on the market mechanism. Let us try to achieve some perspective on the differences—good as well as bad—that distinguish the marketplace as it exists in reality from that of an ideally pure competitive milieu.

Waste

The first effect of market imperfections is clear. It represents a departure from the standards of extreme efficiency promised by pure competition. No longer is every firm producing at the lowest point on its cost curve. No longer are profits minimized. No longer is the consumer the undisputed sovereign of the marketplace. In various forms and guises, waste—useless effort or useless expenditure—is introduced into the system.

Advertising

One form of waste is the enormous proliferation of advertising in an imperfect market society. Today we spend over half as much to persuade buyers to choose this or that brand as we spend for all primary and secondary education—indeed, advertising expenditures can be thought of as a vast campaign to educate individuals to be "good" consumers. Although such an education is quite costly, part of this expenditure may be necessary to stabilize and solidify consumer demand in an affluent society, and some of it certainly has an important informational function or even an enjoyable aspect. After all, if there were no advertising it would be exceedingly difficult for genuine improvements or for new products to make their way into most households. It is probably fair to state that without the possibility of advertising products, the system would lose a great deal of its dynamism.

Yet not all advertising, by any matter of means, conveys information that is genuinely useful to the consumer or introduces new products. It is difficult to contemplate the battles of aspirins, airlines, soaps (up to 10 per cent of the price of soap is accounted for by selling expense), cars, and cigarettes, without recognizing that much of this represents a wastage of scarce resources, including the resources of very gifted and clever people whose efforts are largely directed toward annulling the work of their counterparts in a different advertising agency.

Product differentiation

Waste appears, too, in product differentiation. It has been calculated that the cost to the consumer of annual style changes in cars runs to $5 billion a year or some $700 per car. What the corresponding figures are for other "style" goods, such as the ever-new models of dishwashers and refrigerators, detergents and cosmetics, we do not know. But certainly the prices of many goods could be greatly reduced if a single model were decided on, and all improvements poured into cost reduction. So, too, the resources that must now be spread among competing establishments—the case we mentioned before—"four gas stations" would be much more efficiently employed in one.

The gains from advertising and differentiation

Yet, there are counterarguments. The elimination of brands that assuredly sell the same thing in different packages would leave the question of what policing force would then be left to regulate the one remaining brand. And where product differentiation results in variations in the product itself—and not just in its "image"—one must ask whether the aim of an affluent society is to produce the largest possible quantity of a standardized product at the cheapest possible cost or to offer an array of differing products that please our palates, admittedly at somewhat higher costs. Few consumers in a rich society would prefer an inexpensive uniform to more expensive but highly individualized clothes. From this point of view, even the wasteful parade of car styles has a certain rationale.

Thus, as with advertising, *some* production differentiation plays a useful and utility-increasing function. The question is how much? This is a matter on which it is difficult to form a purely objective judgment, for even if the amount of "useless" product differentiation is relatively small, its impact on the public taste may be disproportionately large. The problem is perhaps particularly acute insofar as much of our "taste" for style seems to be the product of the deliberate advertising efforts of manufacturers. No doubt there is a real aesthetic pleasure in variety, but one doubts that it would take the form of a yearning for "this year's model" without a good deal of external stimulation. Product differentiation thus becomes in part an effort to maximize the public's utilities; but it is also in part an effort to create those "utilities" in order to maximize the producers' profits.

Monopoly and inefficiency

Last, *the wastes of an imperfect market system lie in its inability to push all resources to their point of highest return (and lowest cost).* Every monopoly, large or small, represents a shelter behind which factors are used in lesser quantities than would be the case if the shelter did not exist. Indeed, the whole problem of monopoly is that it prevents the inrush of land, labor, and capital that would take place if there were no barriers to entry.

How serious is the resulting misallocation of resources? Estimates for 1954 give a surprisingly small answer in terms of the aggregate of resources that is blocked out of its point of natural gravitation—perhaps no more than $5 billion—and the effect of transferring this amount of resources would have only a slight effect on the general level of prices. On the other hand, it is also true that profits in monopolistic industries are 50 to 100 per cent higher than those in highly competitive industries: in 1962, for example, the ten largest manufacturing corporations enjoyed profits of 8.7¢ on the sales dollar, whereas the half million corporations doing less than $50,000 of sales each averaged profits of but 3.5¢ per dollar of sales.

The gains from monopoly

Are the higher profits of big business pure waste, like all economic rents? They certainly imply that some prices could be materially reduced. Yet it is difficult to maintain that the high profits of the monopolistic sector have no social utility whatsoever. The handsome factories and offices, the generally more relaxed and generous attitudes toward employees, the growth of fringe benefits and amenities, the prospective transformation of the blue-collar worker into a white-collar salaried employee—all these important evolutionary changes in our economy must also be related to the easier pace and larger earnings of a monopolistic system, rather than to the frenzied pace and penny-pinching attitudes necessitated by a system of full price competition.

More important still, the development of large-scale technologies of low-cost mass production requiring the investment of vast sums, the cultivation of research that cannot possibly "pay off" for years, the restless search for new products that continuously redynamizes the macroeconomy—these attributes of modern capitalism are also by-products of its oligopolistic character and would be impossible to achieve in a regime of atomistic producers.

Waste and the market's operation

Thus, the economic argument of waste is not a simple issue to assess. The gains and losses are difficult to measure and cannot easily be weighed on the same scale. Perhaps it is more useful to ask whether the presence of waste has seriously impeded the operation of the market as a *system*. And here the answer can be given with more assurance. For the forces of the marketplace, although more slowly and sluggishly, continue to press in the *direction* of pure competition.

The pattern of demand, for example, although clearly to some extent the creature of advertising, still retains an independence (if only in the choice of the advertising it believes) that imposes an ultimate authority over the imperfect market. No firm, however large, feels secure in the "possession" of its customers. In the same way, the mobility of firms and factors is badly impeded by market imperfections, but there is nonetheless visible a long-term circulation of land, labor, and capital both among industries and regions: witness the rise of the computer industry, or the decline of rail transportation before the onslaughts of trucking and air travel. And whereas product competition is much less stringent than price competition, it also exerts a slow winnowing effect: of the 100 largest corporations in 1948, nearly a quarter had been displaced from the top (although not, of course, eliminated altogether) by 1960.

Size and instability

Thus the forces of self-interest and of a muted competition still prod the economy in the general direction spelled out by microtheory. But the viscosity of the market in the real world, compared with its extreme fluidity in theory, brings further problems in its wake. Specifically, it endangers the capacity of the market for *self-correction.*

We remember that one of the ways in which the market system assured the orderly provisioning of society was through a complicated chain of price signals and quantity responses—a chain that, as we have seen, brought about larger supplies when prices rose, thereby pressing *against* a further price rise or even rolling prices back; and vice versa when prices fell.

These self-correcting market responses were automatically forthcoming in an environment of small competitive firms who "read" price signals in terms of tomorrow's prospects, but they are by no means so reliable in an environment of giant firms who may ignore price changes entirely (for reasons of sheer bureaucratic inertia) or who may interpret them in a perspective of long-run market strategy. American steel firms, for example, were extremely reluctant to add to steel capacity all through the early postwar period, despite urgent price signals to do so, since they figured (erroneously, as it turned out) that the demand for steel would soon be saturated. As a result, we had a steel "shortage," since the industry neither raised its prices to the equilibrium point (for fear of political repercussions) nor produced enough steel to satisfy the quantity demanded at going prices.

Similarly, the self-correcting market of microtheory takes for granted a flexibility of prices as well as outputs. But big firms and big unions are not eager to allow their prices to fluctuate in response to every change in demand—especially not downward. As a result, market imperfections give us the phenomenon of "sticky" prices. Thus, monopoly elements introduce problems into not only microeconomics but also macroeconomics, by complicating the problem of clearing the market for all goods—that is, making it more difficult to equate the supply of gross national output at *going prices* to the demand for gross national output, without either "gaps" or excesses of demand.

The issue of power

Finally we must come to an issue that is beyond economics proper, but whose roots lie in the facts we have studied and whose importance we must recognize, even if we cannot do it full justice here. This is the problem of power.

We do not study power in pure competition because, as we have seen, the fragmentation of decision making effectively removes it as an economic issue. But the problem cannot be side-stepped in the real market. There the existence of large organizations of labor and capital clearly bring economic power into being, both in terms of an ability of these organizations to secure bigger returns than would be forthcoming under pure competition and in terms of the ability of their massed economic strength to exert influences over the social and political life of the community.

Since market imperfections are not new, the problems of economic power are also not new, and we have been engaged for many decades in trying to control both the sheerly economic and the political and social consequences of bigness. The history of our attempts to do so is written in the antitrust laws, the Taft-Hartley Act, other such legislation, and various regulatory agencies of the government.

How successful have been these efforts to control market-based power? There are many contradictory views. To some, who stress the continued growth of very large-scale business, it seems clear that we have not managed to control business power. To others, seeing the emergence of large labor unions, it is labor power that has eluded effective control. And to still others who are most impressed by the growth of big government, the market has seemed the locus for a growth of public power.

What lies behind this confusion of views is a fact of great importance. *It is that power has emerged in every aspect of economic life as the technological drive of modern society has given rise to large organizations in productive, distributive, and regulatory activity.* Business, labor, and government have *all* participated in this organizational growth, whose roots reach down to the changing technical base of our civilization itself.

As a result, the market is no longer a field in which power is fragmented and disappears, but a setting in which business and labor—and to some extent government—establish their bases of operation. Because the market is itself constantly changing, these bases shift, and power structures built on it are never wholly secure—as we see in the slow turnover of corporate giants or the rise and fall of union strength in different industrial areas or the shift in government power from one regulatory agency to another. In all cases, the market becomes, however, a field of activity to be *organized, administered, regulated,* and *controlled,* whether in the name of business, of labor, or of government.

Given the technological momentum of our time and its continuing tendency to encourage organization, it is doubtful that this trend will disappear. We should expect the appearance of power to constitute a major preoccupation of market-based economies for a long while to come.

Deeper weaknesses of the market system

As we discuss the departures of the real world from the ideal of pure competition, it is well to remind ourselves that the market is not a perfect system, not even in its most idealized form. Out of the striving for profit under the rigors of a competitive struggle emerge not only benefits but disbenefits for the consumer. The grasping employers of the nineteenth century who sweated their children in the textile mills were excellent "economic men." Extremes of riches and poverty, and the differential attitudes of the market to each—solicitous of the rich, indifferent to the poor—are attributes of market systems that must be put into the balance along with the triumphs of productivity and reductions in cost.

A second problem, emphasized by J. K. Galbraith in *The Affluent Society,* is the tendency of a market society to overlook those activities that are not marketable ventures, such as education or the care of the elderly or low-cost housing or public beautification. The contrast, in Galbraith's words, of "private riches and public squalor" must be counted in the ledger across from the mounting totals of GNP.

Third, the market is inadequate to deal with the social consequences of some private action. Thus, when Consolidated Edison Company in New York tots up its annual profits, it does not have to enter a charge for several million dollars worth of cleaning bills—although those cleaning bills (paid by private citizens) are a direct consequence of the smoke that pours out of its chimneys in the course of its profit-making activity. The market, in other words, had no mechanism for correcting—or even for allocating—the *external effects* of private action. In the problems of air and stream pollution, traffic congestion, the ugliness of most Main Streets, we see the price that must be paid for this lack of control.

The market as a social instrument

Thus there are serious weaknesses in the market system—weaknesses that transcend the particular difficulties associated with imperfect competition as such. Essentially the weaknesses stem from the fact that the market has no inherent direction, no internal goal other than to satisfy the forces of supply and demand within it. Such a concern for supply and demand would perhaps be an admirable goal if life were still lived in the relatively self-sufficient and largely rural setting of the nineteenth century, and if the extremes of wealth and poverty were limited. But in a world where wealth is still very lopsided, and where men live totally interdependent lives, crowded into enormous concentrations of cities, the inherent defects of the market bring about very serious deformations.

Yet the very absence of any inherent goals within the market system is also a source of strength. It means that the market is actually a *social instrument* capable of being adapted to, and used for, the achievement of many ends. A society that prefers not to alter the existing distribution of its wealth and income must then allow the market to attain whatever results of production and distribution such a pattern of final demand will impose. But a society that wishes to undertake large-scale social improvements or alterations can also use the mechanism of the market to gain its ends.

In that case, needless to say, it must arrange for a transfer of demand from private to public hands: there must be public buyers able and willing to bid resources into new uses, or there may have to be a diversion of income from those who have a great deal to those who have very little. This public transfer of demand is inherently and inescapably a "command" function, although it may be democratically exercised and controlled. But once the transfer has been made, there is no reason why the operation of the system cannot still be entrusted to the free actions of buyers and sellers on the marketplace, and to competitive vying of profit-seeking firms, each seeking in this case to capture some of the public market rather than confining its activities solely to the private market.

A perspective on the market system

Can we arrive at a final judgment of the strengths and weaknesses of the market system?

Perhaps it is clear by now that there can be no single final judgment—that the market has profound weaknesses and huge strengths, and that it is simplistic to try to make a once-for-all appraisal of such a complex and many-sided social institution.

Rather, in this last word, it seems well to step back from the technical problems of the market and to view it in a larger context of economic history. Then we see the market not merely as an allocatory instrument but as a *social system*—a system that stands in sharp contrast to the systems of tradition and command out of which it emerged, and perhaps in equal contrast to the systems of planning that now characterize so much of the world.

This contrast of systems is by no means haphazard. For if we look again we can see that the great differing means of organizing economic activity bear a relation to the *stage of development* in which societies find themselves. At the beginning of history and at the bottom of the economic ladder (and anachronistically, still present over vast regions of the world) are the systems of tradition by which society pursues its changeless, growthless course. At a later stage in history, and today in those areas of the world that are belatedly recapitulating this history, we find mechanisms of command at work seeking to break the stagnation of tradition and to inaugurate economic progress. As an economic system capable of mobilizing and impelling an entire society (and not merely some small part of it), the market does not appear in history until a long period of transition has been completed and a considerable level of economic growth has been achieved.

Thus the market appears, in the light of history, as a system that is particularly applicable to a certain phase of social evolution—a phase in which the hard trials of the change-over from a stagnant to a growing society have been passed, and when an emphasis on consumption rather than on investment becomes possible. In such an era, when rapid growth at all costs becomes less important than internal flexibility and the satisfaction of consumer demand, the market comes into its own.

And in the future?

If our historical perspective is correct, then we must expect the role of the market to change. For, as we have indicated, the needs and wants of our own society may well be passing beyond the era in which private requirements were to be placed above all other considerations, into a new time when public needs will have to rank as high as, or even above, the demands of the private buyer. If this is so, then we must expect to see the market modified—still used as an instrument of allocation, but no longer constituting in its untrammeled form the end as well as the means of society. This stage of economic history, in which the market will more and more be used for purposes of social planning, is still only in its inception, for we have by no means emerged from the stage of economic history in which the market serves us very well as the originator and the self-guided distributor of our output. Yet there seems little doubt that the cumulative power of economic growth is steadily moving us toward another stage in which the market will be much more the servant and much less the master of the society. Indeed, one would hope that the next great economic achievement of the West would be to meld efficiency and social purpose in a combination that has not yet been reached by an economic society.

Summary

1. The price system of pure competition yields a world in which *economic power is fragmented*. *Demand* (based on utility), *supply* (based on disutility and cost), and *productivity are the three underlying forces of the system*. The firm must accept

their dictates and can in no way impose its own will upon them. Thus, in a world of pure competition, the public becomes the repository of most economic power. This is the meaning of the *"sovereignty of the consumer."*

2. In a world of pure competition, *efficiency is maximized.* This is because each firm is forced, under the threat of its elimination, to combine factors in the way that will lead to the lowest possible unit cost. At the same time, the market also forces each firm to assign its factors to their point of highest marginal return and to pay them the full value of their marginal contribution to output.

3. The world of pure competition exists mainly in theory. To achieve it would entail a *massive breakup of large firms, the end of all barriers to economic mobility, the abolition of brand names,* and so on. This is obviously impossible, even if it were desirable.

4. There are several main consequences of the imperfect market that exists. One is *waste.* We see waste, in part, in advertising, some of which is merely economic effort to nullify other economic effort. Waste is also visible in *product differentiation,* in particular when the "demand" for differentiation is deliberately created. Finally, waste lies in the *failure of the system to push resources to their point of highest return,* because of monopolistic elements in the system.

5. There are some compensating gains from the wasteful elements. Advertising brings *information,* product differentiation brings *variety,* size brings *efficiency* and a more relaxed pace of economic life. And the slow currents of the change that make a market system work are still visible in a reduced but nonetheless effective competitiveness and mobility.

6. Another problem created by imperfection in the market is that of a *lessened capacity of the market for self correction.* This can result in a failure of the market to clear, in the generation of "surpluses" or "shortages," and in the *sticky prices* that complicate monetary problems.

7. Last, market imperfections pose the problem of *power*—a problem that does not exist under pure competition. The market now becomes the locus in which large units of business, labor, and government contend for influence.

8. Aside from its imperfections, the market even as an ideal system has its weaknesses. Basically, these stem from the fact that the market has *no goal-orientation,* save to the structure of existing demand. In turn, this structure reflects the existing distribution of wealth, with its historical inequalities. On the other hand, this absence of internal orientation means that the *market system is also capable of being utilized for social planning* as well as for the operation of a laissez-faire system.

Questions

1. What is meant by saying that the ultimate forces of the pure market are product demand, factor supply, and marginal productivity?

2. What is the meaning of "the sovereignty of the consumer" (and of the worker)?

3. In what way does the market society promote efficiency? How would you define efficiency in terms of pure competition?

4. Make a careful list of all the changes you can think of that would be needed if we were to institute a system of perfect competition.

5. What kinds of advertisements are informational? What kinds are "taste-form-

ing"? Do you think that if there were no ads for cigarettes, smoking would decrease?

6. How much product differentiation do you consider useful? Dress styles? Car models? Laundry soaps?

7. General Motors makes approximately as much profit per car as it pays out in wages per car. Do you think this is intrinsic proof that General Motors earns quasi rents? Monopoly profits? That its costs are lower than those of its competitors? Do you think that the question is answerable? How would you go about answering it?

8. What kinds of actions on the part of buyers and sellers are needed to make a market self-correcting (that is, to enable it to establish equilibrium prices)? In what way do oligopolies or unions interfere with the mechanism of self-correction?

9. What are some of the problems inherent in a "perfect" market? Will a perfect market produce public as well as private goods? How will it deal with the effects of "externalities" such as overcrowding or pollution or traffic congestion?

10. In what way could the market system be used to achieve public goals such as urban rebuilding? Why would it probably be more efficient to use the market as a means of allocating resources to public ends than to have a central direction of resources to the same ends?

Index

I

M

K

L

N

O

P

Q

R